#iranelection

#iranelection

*Hashtag Solidarity and the
Transformation of Online Life*

NEGAR MOTTAHEDEH

stanford briefs
An Imprint of Stanford University Press
Stanford, California

Stanford University Press
Stanford, California

Printed on acid-free, archival-quality paper

Printed and bound in Great Britain by
Marston Book Services Ltd, Oxfordshire

Library of Congress Cataloging-in-Publication Data

Mottahedeh, Negar, author.
  #iranelection : hashtag solidarity and the transformation of online life /
Negar Mottahedeh.
     pages cm
  Includes bibliographical references.
  ISBN 978-0-8047-9587-6 (pbk. : alk. paper)
  1. Iran—History—Election protests, 2009. 2. Presidents—Iran—
Election—2009. 3. Social media—Political aspects—Iran. 4. Internet
and activism—Iran. 5. Citizen journalism—Iran. I. Title. II. Title:
Hashtag Iran election.
  DS318.9.M67 2015
  324.955'061—dc23

                                                        2015014230

ISBN 978-0-8047-9673-6 (electronic)

Typeset by Classic Typography in 10/13 Adobe Garamond

FOR RANJI AND REBECCA

C O N T E N T S

@negaratduke #iranelection RT   1

I   H A S H T A G :   #CNNfail & the slogans of the
2009 Iranian election crisis   9

The Urform 16   "Independence, Freedom, Iranian
Republic" 18   #8Mordad 21   "Down with the Shah!" 24

II   M E M E : YouTube & the telephone call to the beyond   33

Plug In 38   Google YouTube 40   ▬▬▬▬▭ 43
Country: Worldwide 47   Advanced Settings 50
"Allah-o-Akbar" 54   The Urform 60

III   S E L F I E :   Solidarity & everyday life   65

Select & Crop 68   Filter 69   Write a Caption 72
#16Azar 73   #IamMajid 77   #selfie 81   The Urform 83
#tbt 86   #hairdone 93   #instalove 97   #solidarity 99

Acknowledgments   105
Notes   111
Further Reading   135

#iranelection

Women gathered at a rally at the Heidarnia stadium in Tehran, Iran, on Tuesday, June 9, 2009, dressed in green, the color of the Mousavi campaign. (© AP Photo/Ben Curtis)

A sense of euphoria and unprecedented freedom dominated national politics during the presidential campaigns in Iran in the spring of 2009. In the course of the thirty-year history of the theocratic state, no one could remember another time when Iranian state television had broadcast such lively debates among the presidential candidates. Leaving a rally for the sitting president, Mahmoud Ahmadinejad, *Time* magazine correspondent Joe Klein described a crowd of tens of thousands: "They began to filter in to downtown," he recalled. The Ahmadinejad rally was ending around the time that the reformist leader Mir-Hossein Mousavi's rally too was finishing up. Mousavi's supporters made their way downtown, flooding the streets and squares. The scene, as Klein recalled it with obvious awe, was one of camaraderie, of playfulness. Describing the intermingling of the two camps, Klein observed, "they were just kind of joking with each other. It seemed as if someone had opened a magic door and an entire country had spilled out." There was this sense of electricity and excitement. In these days of anticipation leading to the presidential election, people danced in the streets, women and men played around with their outfits, piling up headgear, tying things here and there. Public space felt celebratory and alive and the air was spiked with a flavor of exhilaration. Things were about to change.

1

This wasn't just a feeling. Things looked lively too. Color was everywhere. Election activities were color coded. Campaign paraphernalia, campaign headquarters, and campaigners themselves were clearly differentiated using predesigned graphic coding based on the colors of the candidate's campaign. The incumbent president's supporters used the Iranian flag as their symbol. From the headquarters of Ahmadinejad's main challenger, Mir-Hossein Mousavi, campaigners handed out flyers and posters that were washed in the color green.[1] Voters spoke of Tehran in campaign colors, even as ranking members of the Revolutionary Guard cautioned against rogue groups creating "a colorful" "velvet revolution."[2]

It was during one of the presidential debates that the reformist candidate Mir-Hossein Mousavi had put on a green shawl. The tint of the shawl, an iridescent green, the color assigned to the family of the Prophet, highlighted Mousavi's status as a descendent of the Prophet Muhammad and emphasized his position as the candidate who promised to bring the nation back to the basics, that is, to the original principles of the state as established by the venerated leader of the Islamic Republic, Ayatollah Ruhollah Khomeini, after the 1978 Revolution and, too, back to the traditions of radical kinship founded on Shi'ism's ties to the family of the Prophet through the Twelve Imams.[3]

On June 12, 2009, Iranians went to the polls to elect a new president. Mahmoud Ahmadinejad was reelected as the sixth president of the Islamic Republic of Iran with 63% of the votes cast. Millions believe that their vote was never counted. Final numbers had been announced before the polls were even closed. Thus, a month after Mousavi's appearance on state television, that is, on the days following the election, an all-embracing movement donning green armbands, finger-bands, and headbands took to the streets to call Ahmadinejad's victory a fraud. The color green became the symbol of the opposition.

Images of masses of people filling the vast boulevards, squares, and bridges of the Iranian cityscape were posted to Twitter and

Facebook within minutes. Digital images framed groups of men and women donned in green and black, in headgear or scarves, with one simple question printed by hand on a single sheet of paper: "Where is my Vote?"

Eyewitnesses uploaded videos to YouTube showing a moving sea of millions. They were posted with singular descriptors— "Today" or a mere date—as if the fog of what had just taken place had in some gesture of synesthesia also robbed people of their voice. But the "silent" hum of the crowds in the videos themselves—a hum akin to what you hear in crowded spaces, say, in the bazaar, or a Tehran café—was a hum of intimacy: a refusal to speak to a state that could not be recognized as one's own, a refusal to submit to injustice, a refusal to participate in the co-optation of those whispered words by intruders and opportunists. In this quiet intimacy, future marches were planned and shared: "Tomorrow, there."[4]

Digital images framed older women in a posture of prostration at the feet of the police or holding signs that faced away from the camera. These too spoke of a refusal to relate to the state. Who stood there right next to you was who mattered. Hundreds of such images circulated from within the crowds. Protestors were alternately holding hands and flashing victory signs. Close-ups of men and women, people of different generations and backgrounds, next to each other, marching behind one another: the urgency with which the images were uploaded, shared, studied, commented on, and retweeted established a sense of simultaneity and solidarity. The opposition movement was lovingly embraced online as the "Sea of Green," the "Green Movement," or the "Green Wave." Twitter was awash and enfolded in green.

In these moments of deafening silence from the ground, netizens loudly cautioned against violence, tweeting and posting quotes by the Persian poet Sa'di, by Mahatma Gandhi and Martin Luther King Jr., and by the American author Henry David Thoreau, well known for his essay on civil disobedience.

The silence of the street protestors was broken as the violence of the regime became palpable. A twenty-six-year-old woman, Neda Agha-Soltan, was brutally shot and murdered by the state paramilitary *basij* in Tehran on June 20, 2009, a week after the election. She was not the first martyr of the 2009 uprising.[5] But Neda's death stood out. It had all the imprints of martyrdom, of a corporal act of witnessing, of sacrifice to the secular mind. Her death in the midst of a small group of protestors and friends was captured on a handheld device and immediately uploaded. The digital video documenting Neda's death circulated first on Facebook, then on Twitter. She was described in lengthy comments that accompanied the video as an innocent bystander who curiously led her music teacher into a crowd of peaceful protestors. This textual anchoring of the video created an aura of angelic innocence around her. An injustice had been done. Hundreds of thousands of people watched the video online and reposted it. The video of a young Iranian woman's agonizing death went viral in a matter of hours. Her name, "Neda" ("voice" or "calling" in Persian), became the rallying cry for the Iranian opposition.

Images of the spectacular crowds in green and the viral video of the murdered Neda Agha-Soltan galvanized people of all backgrounds and ages. On Twitter these images linked to and circulated with the hashtags #SeaofGreen, #SoG, #GR88, #Neda, #FreeIran, and #iranelection. Facebook friends created photosets, and personal Flickr accounts were used to archive images that were being posted by way of TwitPic and yfrog onto Twitter's early textual platform[6]—images of the wounded, of women creating barricades, of protestors being assaulted on a street corner, of men carrying rocks, of rows of riot police lining the street, of protective fires large and small, of the *basij* (the state militia) holding cameras and handheld weapons on motorcycles approaching a scattering crowd, of circulating currency stamped in green ink, of an older man being cornered in a doorway by members of the Revolutionary Guard, of a woman wrapped in a black chador attempt-

Supporters of defeated Iranian presidential candidate Mir-Hossein Mousavi rescue an injured riot policeman from the crowd during a protest in Valiasr Street in Tehran on Saturday, June 13, 2009. (© Behrouz Mehri AFP/Getty Images)

ing to rescue someone from being beaten by three *basiji*s, of a young man tying a green finger-band on his female friend's finger, of one hand clasping another in a gesture of kinship.

Images and videos also circulated of protestors rescuing members of the Iranian security forces, those fallen on duty or injured in the midst of the moving crowds. Shielding the riot police from the pressure of the mass, the protestors protectively moved the police off urban boulevards, tended their wounds, and gave them water to drink. Favorited and Liked and in some instances allegorized, these digital documents of solidarity were vigorously downloaded, reposted, and retweeted.

Around the world thousands of "tweeps"—a portmanteau of "Twitter peeps," as the intimate group of early adopters called one another—placed a green overlay on their avatars and changed their time and geolocation to Tehran to stand as alibis in solidarity with those actually tweeting from Iran. They rapidly worked to locate safe houses on Google Maps as news emerged that wounded protestors were being arrested immediately upon their arrival at hospitals. The Australian, Dutch, Mexican, Norwegian, British, German, Belgian, Slovenian, and Portuguese embassies opened their doors to the wounded until there too the assumed protestors were arrested at the gates. Netizens with technical know-how also supported Tor and the newly established NedaNet to secure proxies as news arrived that Iranians were being blocked from the internet and that those with high phone usage (indicating high internet usage) were being identified and arrested.

Posted as status updates and tweets, some of the latest slogans were accompanied with commentaries and translations, others, with peals of laughter. A simple printed sheet of paper: "Look how loud are howls of silence." Graffiti on a city wall: "Down with the dictator." And recalling the first wave of arrests at Tehran University, the day after the presidential election: "Evin prison: Now admitting students."[7]

It was clear from the difference in the frequency of updates only ten days after the election that netizens were glued to their digital screens. American high school students were talking about "Going Iranian" against authority figures.[8] And Western journalists who had been forced to leave Iran during the early days of protest felt bereft and wrote about "the responsibility of bearing witness."[9] Hundreds of songs dedicated to Neda in English and in Persian were uploaded to YouTube and circulated on Twitter and Facebook. Photosets from the early days of the protests were put to 1960s protest songs, and to revolutionary chants borrowed from other parts of the world, many of them revibed by the Iranian student movement.[10] It was indeed a moment when, in the prescient words of W. B. Yeats, "the world bore witness."[11] There was a burst of emotional connectivity, of creativity, of collaboration and exchange in response to Neda's death. Her name became a search topic and a hashtag on Twitter, #Neda. It was the highest-ranking hashtag on June 20, 2009, indicating tens of thousands of posts on the day of her death.

With more than ten thousand #iranelection tweets an hour throughout the month of June, the involvement of netizens in the crisis in Iran was so widespread that the hashtag #iranelection remained the highest-ranking global hashtag on Twitter for two weeks following the presidential election, dropping only momentarily after the unexpected death of Michael Jackson. His death created the largest spike of text message traffic in history, 60% above the average according to AT&T, who reported four million text messages a minute.[12] On Twitter, #MJ overwhelmed every feed. It was inevitable, though, given a whole generation's absolute devotion to Michael Jackson in defiance of the Iranian morality police, that the mashups that were created of this moment of confluence would be not only appropriate but humorous and plentiful. Of the most reposted #MJ #iranelection videos that were made on the occasion of Michael Jackson's sudden death, his

The music of Michael Jackson's "Beat It!" accompanies an image of the Supreme Leader Ayatollah Khamenei. Still from a YouTube video created by YouTube user mydorood. (*Source:* https://www.youtube.com/watch?v=UxIYc9dXT7o)

"Beat It," to the image of the Supreme Leader Ayatollah Khame-nei, and a collage video of the protests on the ground to "They Don't Really Care about Us" were the most popular.[13] The hashtag #iranelection surged again and trended on the thirtieth anniversary of the hostage crisis, on November 4, 2009, and on the thirty-first anniversary of the Islamic Republic, on February 11, 2010, as protests continued on the ground.

Urgent, unjust, and lengthy, the Iranian postelection crisis galvanized and transformed the ecology of life online such that the tropes of #iranelection, its aggregation of an international mass movement around a uniform global hashtag, its valuation of standing "friend/follower" networks and citizen reporting, its engagement with avatar activism, its relentless and conscientious circulation of digital images, its immediate retweeting of the most recent YouTube videos, its hacks, memes, and viral transmissions, its mass participation in flash mobs and text-the-regime campaigns, became part of a sensing, breathing, collective body, part flesh, part data, connected across the globe by way of a continual exchange of digital sights and sounds on social media.

I HASHTAG: #CNNfail & the slogans of the 2009 Iranian election crisis

The figure of the citizen journalist was born out of the glitches of the Iranian postelection crisis of 2009. A series of missteps gave birth to it, and the hashtag #CCNfail presided over the early moments of its birth as a global phenomenon.[1] #CNNfail was associated in the first days of the Iranian protests with the hashtag #iranelection. It was used by Twitter subscribers to underscore CNN's documented failure to report a people's uprising.[2] Recognizing the state of emergency, tweets expressed concern that CNN may have just shut down for the weekend. Instead of reporting on the revolt of a people against the injustices of a state, CNN was looping stories about a meth lab run by a grandmother in Nevada, about the surprising number of complaints around the disappearance of analog television, and on the bankruptcy of Six Flags amusement park. CNN's failure was to eschew a report on an international and collective act of popular dissent, in favor of corporate bids for bankruptcy in the United States.[3]

On the ground in Tehran, BBC correspondent John Simpson and a camera operator were briefly arrested after filming the massive protests in the streets the day after the Iranian presidential election,[4] and Jim Sciutto, an ABC News correspondent, said that the police had confiscated a camera and some of his footage. In response, Sciutto started using his cell phone to capture the protests against the election fraud and the police violence that was directed against the protestors.[5] He posted his updates on Twitter.[6] By June 16, foreign journalists started reporting that they were being banned from the protests.[7] And within a week of the election, foreign journalists, Simpson and Sciutto included, would be summarily rounded up and sent home.[8] Others, including the Iranian-Canadian *Newsweek* reporter Maziar Bahari, were imprisoned, some indefinitely.[9]

Reflecting on Andrew Sullivan's active blog posts on the Iranian postelection crisis, one reader wrote: "Reading your blog over the past 30 something hours makes me realize why the [mainstream media] is really finished. I mean, this point has finally hit home. You are blogging real time events, with descriptions, evaluation, analysis, and eye witness accounts. You are gathering information from a myriad of sources and putting it out there for a cohesive message. CNN, NY Times, et al are merely running an article about 'thousands' of protesters. Its a canned message from just a few stale sources. The revolution is definitely on in Iran. And its on in American journalism too."

A real change in the ecology of global media was underway. News stations and newspapers began to rely heavily on social media for their stories during the course of the postelection crisis and CNN would refer its viewers to its online "*iReport*" section to review what it still called "amateur" videos from Iran. CNN International along with a handful of other news outlets, the *New York Times*, the *Guardian Online*, and the *Los Angeles Times* among them, started to regularly provide information that allowed users in Iran to upload videos, images, and other updates. These digital media would then be incorporated as "breaking" in news reports on Iran. Mainstream media outlets adopted, in most instances, new news formats that would prompt the anchor to explain what was being streamed from YouTube on in-studio monitors.[10] The effects of this shift on journalism in general were profound and were also deeply felt in the op-ed pieces being printed in mainstream media around this time.

New York Times journalist Roger Cohen, mourning his loss of access as a foreign journalist, acknowledged in these moments the ascendency of the activist as citizen journalist. In the midst of the crisis he wrote, "Iranians have borne witness—with cellphone video images, with photographs, through Twitter and other forms of social networking—and have thereby amassed an ineffaceable global indictment of the usurpers of June 12. Never again will Ahmadinejad speak of justice without being undone by the Neda Effect."[11]

On June 16, 2009, four days after the election, @persiankiwi tweeted that all foreign visas had been retracted, that most roads were blocked, and that Tehran hotels were under high security to prevent the foreign press from speaking to any Iranians. Though yet unconfirmed, hackers had reportedly infiltrated the Supreme Leader Ayatollah Khamenei's and the reelected president Mahmoud Ahmadinejad's websites. These sites were now down along with IRIB's, the state television's, website. @persiankiwi and his team were now looking for aid from hackers outside the country to hack into additional government sites.[12]

No one really knew who the person behind the Twitter handle @persiankiwi was at the time, but @persiankiwi started tweeting from Tehran with the hashtag #iranelection a day or so after the election results were announced, alternately anguished over getting timed out because of overburdened phone lines,[13] or in absolute wonderment that people had once again taken to the rooftops to raise the call *"Allah-o-akbar!"* or "God is Great!" as he remembered they had done every night during the revolution against the Shah of Iran thirty years earlier. From the rooftops, he reported, they denounced in the same breath the Supreme Leader, the new dictator that now sat in the Shah's place. "2AM," @persiankiwi tweets on June 14, "and people still on roof shouting death to khamenei. a week ago that was unthinkable. people very fed up. want freedom. #Iranelection"

Always hours and sometimes days ahead of verified news, @persiankiwi came to attract tens of thousands of followers in the days that followed. Working with a nomadic group of three to four hackers (and apparently one doctor after one of the team members suffered a terrible injury at the hands of the state militia), armed with several video cameras, CB radios, and at various times numerous phone lines, @persiankiwi remained a reliable source of detailed information about the situation on the ground in Tehran. He continued to provide the coordinates for the opposition's innovative campaigns all over Iran until his sudden disappearance on June 24, 2009.[14]

Among @persiankiwi's preoccupations during his predawn tweets, when the networks were fairly open, was the un-Islamic manner in which protestors were being treated and the inhumanity that was shown by the state as security forces and the paramilitary basij shot at the crowds, choked young children with teargas, axed protestors' bodies, and shoved them, bloody and lifeless, into vans.

Another concern, which like these preoccupations appeared in @persiankiwi's tweets—and that were reflected repeatedly in individual blogs and in the slogans of other protestors—was a resounding concern over Iran's state media.[15] Despite the presence of hundreds of thousands of protestors in the streets, state radio and television persisted in covering up the protests. Not only was state television refusing to report on the uprising; it was broadcasting lies about the discrepancies in the election results, and running sitcoms and miniseries to create a lull in the citizenry.

The most obvious symptom of the state media's cover-ups were the glitchy screens that faced viewers as they turned to BBC's Persian satellite channel for news on the day of the election, and for the weeks following.[16] The pixelated compression of parts of the image and sound, which like most software glitches amounted to the deletion of key frames and the algorithmic editing together of two obviously unrelated frames, modified whole broadcasts along the entire footprint of the satellite. Satellite technicians traced the interference immediately. It was clear that the BBC signal was being jammed from Iran.[17] Faces and moving hands were pixelated, and jump cuts stalled the tilting of heads and the movement of bodies and lips on screen. Voices dragged deep and cracked as background footage turned to static and washed out in color. These glitches, which fiercely blocked access to the news, produced an unpredictable change in the ways people connected across the boundaries of states, and affected the transmission of information between large networks of people online and off. This transformation in the media environment affected the ecology of global *life*.

The fact that the Iranian state media was lying about the protests, combined with the glitchy screens that faced viewers when they turned to the news, required of those witnessing the uprising in Iran to provide the world with evidence. In the digital videos that citizens uploaded, masses of people appeared in green ribbons, bound neatly around their wrists and their fingers; digital

Protestors occupy city streets and squares after the announcement of the election results on June 12, 2009. (CC by 2.0. Faramarz Hashemi, www.flickr.com/photos/fhashemi/. Photo originally circulated on TwitPic, June 2009)

devices held aloft, they captured the moments of the uprising for others, *as their collective eyes and ears.* Bodies and devices moved effortlessly amid fluid crowds. In images that went viral within minutes of being posted, protestors were framed sitting cross-legged and bravely in front of the shields of the riot police and the state's security forces. They were sitting in protest with faces covered; in dark sunglasses; in the heat of the summer. They appeared on rooftops and moved in waves that washed entire boulevards in bodies of green and black, where a single sheet of hand-printed paper asked: "Where is my Vote?"

On June 18, 2009, six days into the crisis, @persiankiwi tweeted at the state media:

> IRIB.ir - How is it possible that 2Million people march in your country and you say NOTHING? #iranelection 3:48 AM - 18 Jun 2009

The alarm over the lies that were being broadcast by the state media about the election, about the protests and the violence of the security forces, began to overshadow concern about the election results, on the streets and online too. On June 23, 2009, Homa Maddah a twenty-six-year-old protestor wrote in a *Tehran Avenue* blog, "the state radio and television is no longer the place where worthless sitcoms and mini-series, unimportant news items and sports news are broadcast, it is that 'demi-monster' that comes out of hiding every night and through lies and fiction tries to scare us."[18]

Six years earlier in 2003 when demonstrations against the privatization of Iran's universities broke out at the University of Tehran, Iranian state television and radio had shown itself similarly unwilling to report on the developments. At best, it was a source of misinformation. As one eyewitness notes, it was the Iranian satellite channels broadcasting from Los Angeles that showed the images from the protests at the university in Tehran: "On the foreign channels—people sent video from here [Tehran] and through the Internet. There was also video footage online, of the beatings, the raids, they showed the protests—they showed video footage of the protests and were broadcasting it. Here on the [domestic] news they didn't show the protests at all. Like, two or three days later they just said that at night, a bunch of hooligans raided the university dorm."[19] In contrast to Iranian state television, the Persian-language satellite channels in the diaspora tracked the 2003 protests around the clock. They continuously took calls from eyewitnesses and streamed digital videos from the protests.

Using these, they substantiated claims of state violence. This interactive method of communication and urgent mediation of breaking news, which by going abroad in order to broadcast nationally actively sought ways to bypass state media and the Iranian cyber army's regular filtering and hacking of blogs and opposition websites, was to become the blueprint for the global engagement of social media in the 2009 Iranian postelection crisis.

In 2009, the figure of the citizen journalist emerged globally in the first weeks of the Iranian uprising from within the glitches on

A television set held aloft at a postelection demonstration. The text reads, "Lying media!" (*Source:* http://imgdex.com/1628)

the screens of international satellite broadcasts and the outraged cries of #CNNfail on Twitter. The citizen journalist was a configuration, part flesh, part data. Connected to the protesting crowds on the ground and her followers and friends online, her slogan was a hashtag: a resounding #iranelection. The efficiency of her delivery to her networks online was contrasted to mainstream media and thematized on all platforms, from the tweet to the *iReport*, on international blogs and on city streets everywhere.

Allegorizing the birth of the cyborgian citizen journalist, an actual television box appeared on the streets of Tehran balanced overhead in a march towards IRIB, the state radio and television headquarters. Printed on each of its sides was this slogan: "Lying Media!"[20]

THE URFORM

To begin this book with the hashtag is to begin with an object that was itself revolutionized in the first months of the 2009 Iranian postelection uprising. The hashtag was from its origins a keyword, a form of tagging that would give meta-information about content and provide a system of classification for materials online and for internet relay chats (IRC). Within networks it was used to label groups and topics. First introduced into the microblogging environment Twitter in 2007 by Chris Messina[21] as a way to create groups, the hashtag became an aggregator, a way to search a topic, and by bringing focus and attention to posted content, a way to measure the range and popularity of a topic on the social media platform. It was one effort, among many, to master the overwhelming transmissions of the digital age.

#iranelection emerged on Twitter as the markup for the most retweeted posts on current events in Iran. Thus during the first weeks of the crisis, the hashtag went from being a localized practice among smaller groups on Twitter to becoming an international practice in writing posts more generally. Four days after the election, *Mashable* reported that subscribers on Twitter had produced 221,744 tweets per hour about Iran on June 16, with over

22,500 tweets per hour dedicated to the hashtag #iranelection alone.[22] #iranelection was the first long-trending international hashtag in Twitter's history. Recognizing its utility, Twitter placed current trending hashtags next to users' streams in the early days of #iranelection. Then, in the early months of 2010, the platform made a decision to hyperlink hashtags within tweets and introduced trending topics to its front page.[23]

Precisely because access to social media is now ubiquitous, the implications of the uses of social media are often assumed today without further reflection. Social media platforms' current forms and functions are thus retrospectively projected back onto earlier incarnations and functions. We forget that it was in these very moments of crisis that the hashtag (#iranelection) as a networked aggregator of texts, images, videos, audio recordings, and URL links effectively forged a communal sensorium, that is, eyes and ears that were shared by protestors on the ground and netizens online, simultaneously transmitting, indeed creating and living a shared international experience. In the most critical moments of the historical uprising, bodies and social media handles effectively became memes, viral transmitters of packages of content, of sensory experiences, and of actions that in their simultaneous expression around a long-trending hashtag fundamentally impacted the function and purpose of media platforms such as Twitter, Facebook, Google, and YouTube. The solidarity that took shape around the first-ever international hashtag, #iranelection, situated the continuity between the corporal senses and a communal one that was shared by a multitude on the social media platform. The hashtag itself produced a collective sensorial solidarity online in an age where contemporary political and economic ecologies under the aegis of governmental and corporate neoliberal policies seemingly move towards eliminating the possibilities of assembly for groups, unions, cooperatives, and collectives on the ground everywhere. This international solidarity, an overpowering sense of affinity and kinship, among netizens and protestors on the ground, was what shaped the forms and functions of social media platforms as we recognize them today.

What becomes clear then as we focus attention on the function of the hashtag is the ways it emerges out of an urform, an ancient incarnation, which is that of the slogan. During the Iranian election crisis, posts often ended with "#iranelection RT RT RT." True, the hashtag #iranelection was an aggregator of the thousands of posts that were tweeted on the topic per second, but in the call to RT RT RT (retweet, retweet, retweet) that appeared in virtually every early post on Twitter, the hashtag itself crystallized into a slogan: an urform resurrected, reanimated, and redeemed just as the slogans of the "Sea of Green" were being quelled on the street and forced onto rooftops and balconies in the darkness of the night.

It was not altogether surprising, then, that hashtags in tweets would be hyperlinked during this rather brief period in the history of online life, allowing users on Twitter to connect one poster's tweet with another's. The hashtag became the sign and symbol of a collective demand. #iranelection as both an aggregator of a long-trending topic and the repeated slogan of netizens would come to be the marker of a global solidarity and the uprising of one people united against injustice.

"INDEPENDENCE, FREEDOM, IRANIAN REPUBLIC"

In his monograph on the slogans of the Islamic Revolution, Muhammad Hossein Panahi remarks that the 1978 Revolution in Iran with its four thousand slogans is a unique case among revolutions. No other revolution has produced anything close to these numbers. The 1917 Russian Revolution had twenty-eight slogans, the 1789 French Revolution had twenty-three, the Communist Revolution in China had thirty-five.[24]

Perhaps the most memorable chants of the Iranian Revolution are the ones that made their appearance on the streets of Tehran on September 4, 1978, to mark the end of the month of fasting, the month of Ramadan.

Florists handed out carnations, and protestors marched with flowers to the Shah's army, chanting, "O military brother, why are you killing your brother?" When on December 28, 1978, the Shah's army opened fire on the funeral cortege for a twenty-seven-year-old professor killed the day before, the crowd seized on a young soldier on 24 Esfand Square. We know 24 Esfand Square today as Enqelab Square (Revolution Square).

On Monday, June 15, 2009, less than three days after the presidential election in Iran, thousands gathered to rally at Azadi Square (Freedom Square). The militia opened fire at the crowd, killing at least thirteen protestors and injuring many more. Spontaneously, the crowd raised the bodies of those murdered on Freedom Square and broke into a chant: "*Mikosham, Mikosham anke baradaram kosht*" (I will kill, I will kill, he who killed my brother) —a chant that first appeared during the demonstrations on Black Friday (17 Sharivar), September 8, 1978.

This chant, and the crowd's associated gesture, not only recalled the 1978 revolutionary slogans directed at the Shah's army, "our military brothers," but, too, retrieved the chants of the young soldiers who defended Iran against invasion in the long war against Saddam Hussein's Iraq between 1980 and 1988. Nesting in the branches of this chant is a recollection that brings home, in the midst of the 2009 postelection crisis, the profound betrayal by the state and its paramilitary of the Islamic Republic's founding ethics of radical kinship and solidarity.

The slogan "Independence, Freedom, Islamic Republic" was first chanted during the march on September 4, 1978, that opposed the Iranian monarchy. The march was the most massive demonstration against the Iranian monarchy up to this point, and people were invited to participate in another demonstration four days later in Southern Tehran.[25] That day, September 8, 1978, would be remembered as "Black Friday," a turning point in the history of the Iranian Revolution. Citizens were no longer willing to stand back as the resources of the nation were depleted by the ruling monarch and his Western allies. What they claimed they wanted, at every turn, was an ideal; a utopia that one might call, in the phraseology of the grand Ayatollah who was to replace the monarch, "an

Islamic government," which by all accounts would go beyond establishing a mere theocracy.

Having spoken to many students, religious teachers, and intellectuals in Tehran and Qum, Michel Foucault who was eager to understand the nature of this collective aspiration, concluded that this utopian ideal was at its core a complex web of time and space, the site of a spatiotemporal confluence. This ideal was, at once, "something very old and also very far into the future, a notion of coming back to what Islam was at the time of the Prophet, but also of advancing toward a luminous and distant point where it would be possible to renew fidelity rather than maintain obedience." "In pursuit of this ideal," Foucault concluded, "the distrust of legalism seemed to me to be essential, along with a faith in the creativity of Islam."[26]

From his exile in France, Ayatollah Ruhollah Khomeini "sent out his appeal to the students." In sermons recorded and circulated on cassette tapes, he addressed "the Muslim community and the army," too, cautioning against any negotiations with the current dictator, the ruling monarch, Mohammad Reza Shah Pahlavi.[27]

And there it was, as Foucault had observed it in October 1978, palpable across the thousands of miles that separated France from Iran: a powerful, "mysterious current . . . flowed between an old man who had been exiled for fifteen years and his people, who invoke his name."[28] Making famous Frantz Fanon's critical phrase "the wretched of the earth," a phrase that Iranian modernists had translated as *mostaz'afin*, Khomeini rallied people of different classes, ethnic groups, and political affiliations around the quest for social justice for the nation. In Fanon, this call for "a new form of the nation," as Ranjana Khanna argues, was "equally a call for a psychical structure."[29] Khomeini's radical mobilization of a people that had, by most accounts, been turned into a "rotting mass" by a West-oriented monarchy, was exhilarating. "Even Foucault took a megaphone to the streets of Tehran," writes Roxanne Varzi:

> He, like everyone else, was mesmerized by the new leader who quickly led a disparate group of Marxists, feminists, socialists, radical Islamists,

secular students, and everyday citizens into one cry: "*Allah-o Akbar*," "God is great."[30]

The people's revolution was relentless and insurrectionary. The ruling monarch, Mohammad Reza Shah, fled the country the following January, and the future spiritual and political leader of the country, Ayatollah Ruhollah Khomeini, arrived from his exile in Paris to a joyous crowd of five million on February 1, 1979. He called for a general election. And in March 1979, Iranian national television reported that 98% of Iranians had cast their vote in a referendum in favor of the establishment of the Islamic Republic. The report showed Iranians at the polls with placards calling for "*Esteghlal, Azadi, Jomhouri Eslami*" (Independence, Freedom, Islamic Republic).[31]

It was also during the demonstrations of September 4, 1978, the same protests in which the demand for an Islamic Republic was first formulated in the form of a slogan, that "the crowds renamed major landmarks. Pahlavi Avenue became Mossadeq Avenue, Eisenhower Avenue became Freedom Avenue, and Shahyad (literally 'the Shah's memorial') became Freedom Square."[32] This renaming took place as the processions wound through Tehran's city streets and as the protestors established their opposition to the Pahlavi monarchy.[33]

It was on these same streets and squares—Freedom Avenue and Revolution Square—that the call for "Independence" and "Freedom" for Iran reappeared thirty years later, on July 30, 2009, in the slogans of the opposition. It appeared this time in a slightly altered form. Here, not far from Revolution Square, a considerable crowd of protestors raised their voices and chanted the slogan that would undercut the foundations of the Revolution itself: "Independence, Freedom, Iranian Republic."[34]

#8MORDAD

The July 30, 2009, protests, coinciding with the eighth day of the Persian month of Mordad (8 Mordad), marked the fortieth day of mourning for the death of Neda Agha-Soltan and the other martyrs of the 2009 uprising. The fortieth is a significant day of commemoration in accord with Shi'ih traditions of mourning. Thousands gathered at the Beheshteh-Zahra Cemetery. The many martyrs of the Iranian Revolution were buried here, alongside those who had died in the first days of the 2009 crisis. The Beheshteh-Zahra Cemetery, renamed by some protestors after Neda's death the Beheshteh-Neda Cemetery,[35] is historically significant as the site of Ayatollah Khomeini's first address to the people. Here at the Beheshteh-Zahra, he immediately laid out his vision for the Iranian film industry and the media.

On July 30, 2009, one eyewitness reported that upon arriving at the cemetery, their driver "half-jokingly" asked the police officer on guard what was going on at the cemetery. "Nothing," answered the officer, "just go to row 257," identifying in the enormous cemetery, flanked with avenues and squares, Neda's own gravesite where people had been slowly gathering to honor her unthinkable death.[36] Later that day, row 257 became the site of further confrontations with the security forces and, perhaps not unironically, the site of the arrest of two prominent filmmakers, Jafar Panahi and Mahnaz Mohammadi.[37] Mohammadi, a documentary filmmaker known for her work in women's cinema, was charged and imprisoned on the grounds of espionage and collaboration with the BBC (a charge she vehemently denies). Panahi, whose first feature film, the *White Balloon*, won the 1995 Caméra d'Or at the Cannes Film Festival, was given a six-year sentence and banned from filming and travel for the next twenty years.

Early images and videos streaming from the cemetery and from gatherings of five hundred or more people in small pockets of protest all over Tehran were notable for the almost total absence of the police and the security forces. The atmosphere was electric. New slogans were being chanted. They were cutting and to the point: "*Khamenei ghatel-e, velayatesh batel-e!*" (Khamenei is a murderer, his leadership is null and void!); "*Estefa, Estefa! Dolateh coup d'etat!*" (Resign, resign, coup government!). Commentators were brimming with excitement. Protestors were calling for an end to the theocracy and demanding an Iranian Republic!

Such slogans as vehicles for the demands of the opposition were taking on the character of evidence in political debates online, on Iranian satellite channels, and in mainstream media as journalists shared their opinions on the unfolding events from some distance away. Their arguments were convincing but ultimately injudicious and premature.[38]

By Quds Day (Jerusalem Day), on September 18, 2009, it was clear from the movement of the people through streets whose very names bore witness to a revolutionary uprising only a generation earlier, combined with the sheer number of slogans being generated, and the multitude of chants citing, but more importantly, reversing the terms of the Revolution's slogans, that these untimely conclusions in the media were missing the powerful cultural transformations that were taking place in Iran. What we were witnessing was a revolution, but this revolution was taking place under the skin.

Quds Day is held in the Muslim world on the last Friday of the month of Ramadan, the month of fasting. *Quds* is the Arabic name for *Jerusalem*. Thus, Quds Day was originally envisioned by Ayatollah Khomeini as a day when Muslims everywhere come together to voice their unity and take a stand "against the Zionist occupation of Israel." Quds Day is a call to solidarity with the Palestinian people against injustices heaved at the Muslim world.

In Tehran, the state-organized Quds Day demonstrations on September 18, 2009, took on the posture of a general strike by systematically reversing the terms of the old revolutionary and normative state chants. The protests began at 10 A.M. at Haft-e Tir (7 Tir) Square, and those in attendance were hailed by government loudspeakers to repeat the customary slogans of the day: "Down with America!" "Down with Israel!"

By this time, the opposition had been protesting Mahmoud Ahmadinejad's fraudulent reelection to the presidency for almost three months. Israel and America were not the immediate concern.

Ahmadinejad had traveled to Russia for a summit of the Shanghai Cooperation Organization on June 16, 2009, just days after the election. Russian government officials saw this visit as a sign of a hopeful advance in Russian-Iranian relations. Dmitry Medvedev, the Russian president, was among the first world leaders to congratulate Ahmadinejad on his reelection. Meanwhile, the United States and the European Union were insisting that "the who" of the presidency was still in question. On the ground, the protesting crowds were furious. Israel and America were not the enemies. Resistant and disciplined to the core, the crowd disregarded the staged call and response blasting from the government loudspeakers. Their sonorous outrage rung through the streets: "Down with Russia! Down with Russia!"[39]

"DOWN WITH THE SHAH!"

A video documenting this energetic reversal of the officially sanctioned Quds Day slogans was posted on YouTube; it shows the crowds assembled on Karim Khan-e Zand Street in Tehran.[40] According to Mehdi Saharkhiz and the UCLA-based online mapping project Hypercities,[41] the crowds arrived at Karim Khan-e Zand around noon moving in the direction of Valiasr Square.

Some weeks after these protests, I was anonymously forwarded an audio recording that captures the voices of the government's Revolutionary Guard as they reported on the Quds Day demonstrations.[42] Security forces had entered the crowd during the protests (at Karim Khan-e Zand Street) and had requested that the demonstrators not chant so-called political slogans. In other words, the crowds were only to chant the government-sanctioned slogans, which were broadcast over the government-sanctioned loudspeakers. (Coincidentally, these were not considered political slogans.) The government loudspeakers persisted their cry over the voices of the assembled: "Down with America!" "Down with Israel!"[43]

The recording I received opens with two chants: "*Irani mimirad zelat nemipazirand*" (Iranians would rather die than tolerate humiliation), and "*Na Gaza Na Lebnan Janam fadaye Iran*" (Neither Gaza, nor Lebanon, I give my life for Iran). The latter, a strikingly nationalist chant, homes in on the government's concern for Palestine and Lebanon over the lives and liberties of the nation's own citizens. Such sentiments crystallized to underscore the state's betrayal of its own founding ethics when, a few months later, during the government-sponsored anti-American demonstrations on the anniversary of the hostage crisis (November 4), another chant, abhorrently emphasizing the historically fabricated origins of a Persian race, emerged on the streets: "*Nejade ma aryast-deen, az siasat jodas*" (We are an Aryan race, religion and politics don't mix). The denial of kinship with the Arab world in these slogans would repeatedly bow towards a secularism that also distastefully aimed to associate a racially distinct Aryan Iran with the mores of the West.

On the recording, a member of the Revolutionary Guard introduces himself, identifying his location. He is at Boulevard Keshavars (Farmers Boulevard) at its intersection with Felestin (Palestine) Street. Reporting on the crowd, he observes: "It is moving towards Naderi Street. It is chanting, 'Down with the Dictator!' and 'Down with Russia!'"[44] He then goes on to say, "They are wearing green and they are in motion." Asked about the scope of the crowd, he seems unable to respond. The protestors' voices return, "*Doroghgoo, doroghgoo shast-o-se-darsadet ku?*" (Liar! Liar! Where's your 63%?), referring to the percentage of votes claimed by Ahmadinejad in the elections. The officer's voice is once again heard on the recording as he reports that there are "four to five thousand of the Green Wave ..." Recognizing that he has just misspoken, a misstep that reveals his sense of familiarity, or one could say his kinship and connectedness, with the "Sea of Green" moving before him, the Guard corrects himself. Retracing his words, he remarks, "Green Wave supporters are on the move." Reporting from Enqelab (Revolution) Street, another officer refers to the crowd as "*Mowj-e sabz-ha*" (the Green Wavers). "They're gathering and moving towards Revolution Street."

As the crowd arrives at Revolution Street, we hear the call *Allah-o-akbar!* (God is Great!) in the feed.[45] *Allah-o-akbar!* was the defining sound of the 1978 protests against the Shah, when citizens climbed their rooftops nightly to raise a defiant cry. "The shouting and screaming of 'God is Great' became background music for the revelation of outlawed and censured news," Minoo Moallem recalls, "including information about the number of deaths and arrests, as well as the announcement of the date, time, and location of plans for future political demonstrations."[46] In 1978, the Shah's prime minister, Major General Gholam Reza Azhari, attributed these nightly cries of *Allah-o-akbar!* to cassette tapes, claiming "that only a small group of people were responsible."[47] Rather than show a willingness to acknowledge the growing number of dissatisfied citizens, the prime minister referred to mechanical reproductions and cassette recordings, denying in one stroke the thousands upon thousands who climbed the country's rooftops to protest the Shah by calling on the greatness of God: "Those are cassette recordings, not real protestors."

True, the "utilization of microphones and cassettes, along with live voices, created confusion between embodied voices (of the anti-Shah protestors) and those created through mechanical ventriloquism" in the darkly lit skies of those revolutionary nights. Cassette sermons of prominent clerics and of Ayatollah Khomeini himself, too, were known as major agitators during the long months of the Iranian Revolution. Nevertheless, in the final instance it was the will of the people to perpetuate the uprising against the Shah's government. The prime minister's accusations thus prodded a 1978 revolutionary slogan by anti-Shah demonstrators during the first mass demonstrations, in which millions of people showed up to march the streets of Tehran. Referring to the vast number of people marching on the street against his government, the protestors chimed that cassette tapes don't have feet: "*Azhari Goosaleh, Bazam migi navareh? Navar ke pa nadareh!*" (Azhari, you calf, still think it's tape? Tapes don't walk!).[48]

Incorporating this 1978 slogan into the programming of early silent protests in 2009, as if their banners were screen-grabs of obfuscated code, protestors responded to Ahmadinejad's claim that the burgeoning crowd of postelection demonstrators were "riff-raff"[49]—disappointed soccer fans whose team had lost—with this chant: "*Doktor-e Kapshen pareh, khashak ke pa nadare!*" (Doctor with a torn overcoat,[50] riff-raff doesn't walk!).[51] This 2009 slogan against Ahmadinejad playfully unearthed the revolutionary chant against the Shah's prime minister as if it were being mined from the very soil, the brick and mortar of the city streets. For in this span of the thirty years since the Revolution, Tehran, the city, had become a mnemotechnic device, and the objects and sounds that inhabited its collective spaces had inscribed images and echoes that archived its losses and passions: the raised bodies of the dead, the sound of marching feet on pavement—all sensory moments of revolutionary memory. In these mined moments of the city, the literal thresholds between the boulevards and sidewalks appeared to those in motion as "metaphoric" thresholds.[52] In the imaginary of a revolutionary city, one habituated through promenades and recollections, the surfaces of walls and buses appeared as the protestors' desks, "the newspaper kiosk their library, letterboxes their bronze statuettes, benches their boudoir."[53] When masses of people can read the signs of the city collectively as the tale of a passionate revolution, the city harbors within its frame "a density of meanings at once habitual and disjunctive, intersecting past and future, loss and desire, individual recollection and collective unconscious."[54] This mode of reading the city, grounded in the Proustian notion of involuntary memory (the "*memoire involuntaire*"), provided Walter Benjamin with the tools to formulate his theory of the mimetic faculty.

In his work, Benjamin described the mimetic faculty as the ability to produce and perceive similarity or correspondence either consciously or unconsciously. The child, the prime bearer of the mimetic faculty, "not only plays at being a grocer or a teacher, but also at being a windmill or a train," Benjamin muses.[55] There is a revolutionary "signal" that "proceeds 'out of the world in which the child lives and gives commands.'"[56] As Susan Buck-Morss reflects, "[The child's] drawers must become arsenal and zoo, crime museum and crypt. 'To tidy up' would be to demolish an edifice full of prickley chestnuts that are spiky clubs, tinfoil that is hoarded silver, bricks that are coffins, cacti that are totem-poles and copper pennies that are shields." This capacity, the capacity for mimetic improvisation, of perception and active, in-the-moment transformation, proceeds from a revolutionary consciousness in which "new forces and new impulses appear."[57]

In the Quds Day protests of 2009, it was these mimetic gestures of the moving crowds, the protestors' act of perceiving and actively retooling the history of a shared past alongside the ordinary and habitual act of walking the revolutionary streets and squares of the city, that jostled the involuntary memory of the Revolutionary Guard.

On Boulevard Keshavarz, where a crowd of two thousand were spotted, moving in the direction of 16 Azar Street, the reporting officer observes, "They are clapping and chanting, 'Mousavi! Mousavi!'" The report continues as another officer identifies himself, observing: "The crowd is wearing green and is moving from the Northern part of Boulevard Keshavarz. The crowd stretches to Boulevard Felestin." In the background of the recording, the people's voices come in clearly: "*Marg bar Diktator!*" (Down with the Dictator!); "*Range ma, range ma Neda-ye ziba-ye ma!*" (Our color, our color! Our beautiful Neda!/voice!)

The slogans that are reported by the Revolutionary Guard next evoke another era, when in the first major demonstration against the monarchy during the Revolution the crowd called out to their military brothers, inviting them to join forces with them. Here, on Quds Day 2009, the officer reports on a chant, "The real *basijis* were Hemmat and Bakeri," which recalls the names of two heroic commanders of the army who were killed during the eight-year Iran-Iraq War. This slogan also appeared in green ink on circulating banknotes in the summer of 2009. The image that was printed alongside the slogan was a reproduction of a viral photograph showing three members of the state militia pummeling a protestor as a woman in a black chador tries to rescue him. Such was the way of contemporary *basijis* during the election crisis of 2009, a turn against the very people the state militia had defended against Saddam's Iraq a generation earlier.

As the large crowd occupying the northern section of the boulevard and the buildings chants, encoding in this 2009 slogan the eight-year Iran-Iraq War in which thousands died, the Revolutionary Guard's report suddenly falters and trips over itself. The Guard misspeaks: instead of reporting the slogan "Down with the dictator!" which is what the crowd is actually chanting, the officer,

A woman in a chador attempts to rescue a man being beaten by the state militia (*basiji*s) on Sunday, June 14, 2009. (© AP)

Iranian currency stamped with statement, "The real basijis were Hemmat and Bakeri," and added image of *basiji*s (state militia) beating a protestor. (*Source:* http://raymankojast.blogspot .com/2009/11/green-money.html)

recalling the 1978 demonstrations, the Shah, and the demand for his resignation, reports, "They are chanting, 'Down with the Shah!' and 'Resign! Resign!'" retrieving and repeating the chants of a revolution that took place three decades earlier.

In the movement of the crowds through the streets; in the general strike that is induced by the "quotation" of the old revolutionary chants, and then their reversal; in the people's deliberate—and the Revolutionary Guard's involuntary—citation of an earlier era, indeed, of another dictator, what we read in the Quds Day protests are the markers of the unconscious, indeed, the revolutionary current that shapes the everyday life of the collective.

The opposition's gesture of travel, its weaving through the Revolution's renamed streets, its acts of citation and reversal, all bind the protesting crowds and the spaces that they traverse to the revolutionary past. In recollection, this past is neither secular nor religious, and comingled with the past, the present is both. In striking, enacting, and renewing, the crowd moves through streets, squares, and boulevards that are renamed at moments of fiery passion and revolt. Those boulevard names are sealed off, streets cordoned by new names, associated with a historical moment of revolutionary transformation. They are reconnected to a new history and a new generation, powerfully creating the new day.

As the crowd moves through the streets, shoulder to shoulder and face to face with the Revolutionary Guard, chanting, recording, and uploading, it triggers an involuntary memory, not as a collective dream image of a new revolution in which religion and state separate, but as a dialectical image with revolutionary potential. Where voluntary memory would recall events in sequential arrangement, the space of involuntary memory as a space that sees correspondences between the past and the present is characteristically disorderly.[58] The lived everyday of the streets and the deep connectedness of its spaces and histories emerge and manifest unconsciously in the missteps (Freud's parapraxis) of the Revolutionary Guard. These "glitches of the mind" (one could say) reveal the quotidian workings of an unconscious that creatively transforms that which is, through perceived correspondences and past-present constellations. What appears is something other, something new.

Revolutionary because constellated in the shuttle of similarities between the present and the past, this consciousness boils up in the involuntary memory of the Revolutionary Guard in the recording. As the Guard moves with the playful, protesting crowds through the renamed streets of the Iranian capital, memories break through and misspeak the present in the frame of an urgent corresponding past, thus filling up slices of time with messianic and revolutionary potential. The emergence of this shared revolutionary consciousness between the Revolutionary Guard and the "Sea of Green" hinges on the slogans that once transformed Iran's cityscapes in gestures of kinship and solidarity. This consciousness finds correspondences in the geographies of online life. The transformations that took place in the ecology of social media were generated by a similar solidarity, a global solidarity formed around the slogan of the net's first inhabitants—the slogan #iranelection.

II MEME: YouTube & the telephone call to the beyond

A viral poster for an early #iranelection flash-mob campaign announced a mass strike at the grand bazaars in Tehran, Isfahan, Shiraz, Mashhad, Tabriz, and Ahvaz set for August 12, 2009 (21 Mordad, 1388). Sometime earlier, in the early weeks of the Iranian postelection protests, @persiankiwi had tweeted the blueprint for another flash-mob campaign at the bazaar:

> do NOT wear green - dress normally - bring your children - if stopped u are ONLY going shopping #Iranelection 3:09 pm - 23 Jun 2009[1]

The idea of the mass strike in August as announced on the poster was a meme. It was a deliberate genetic copy of the plan tweeted by @persiankiwi in June but with one alteration: take your family to the bazaar at 10 A.M. Go shopping, but don't shop. Completing the viral poster were three words taken from another poster and added to this one. The words read, "*Resaneh Shoma Hasteed*" (You are the media).

These three words, which appeared repeatedly on #iranelection websites, walls, posters, and images, marked a real shift in the

(Opposite) Flash-mob campaign poster. The text reads, "Fellow citizen rise up! Public announcement: Green Shopping. On Wednesday we will all go shopping at the bazaar together. From 10 A.M. Wednesday 21 Mordad. Meet at the Grand Bazaar in Tehran, Shiraz, Mashhad, Isfahan, Tabriz, Ahvaz. We will ask the shopkeepers to stand in solidarity with the people and go on strike. You are the Media. Spread the word!" (*Source:* http://www.iranpressnews.com/)

context of the postelection crisis. To congregate in the streets was too dangerous. The security forces were aggressively engaged and the government's cyber army was monitoring social media. It was hacking accounts and redirecting websites.[2] The state was eager to suppress the opposition's various protests and to restore quiet after the election. Protestors were being tracked, their mobile phones confiscated on the streets. This and the intermittent access to landlines and to stable and secure internet connections made the use of digital and handheld media unpredictable. Protestors themselves had to become the carriers of content. Their status updates and event announcements would have to live *in them*, as they had lived virally on their Facebook walls, and instead of being reposted they would have to be delivered personally to everyone they met. Transformed into a conveyer of viral content, "you" were the media, "you" were the meme.

The word "meme" was introduced by Richard Dawkins as the replicator that conveys imitation by way of gestures, speech, rituals, or other cultural phenomenon; it is an idea, a unit of cultural transmission. Analogous to the gene, the meme self-replicates, mutates, adapts, and responds to external pressures. The internet meme is "a hijacking of the original idea" in Dawkins,[3] in that the copied object of the meme is deliberately altered by creative means and spread through viral transmission. "Genes are replicators [that] make accurate copies," argues Dawkins. "Memes are the other kind of replicators. Memes spread through human culture as genes spread through the gene pool. Memes [are] good ideas, [like] good tunes. Anything that spreads by imitation as genes spread by reproduction or bodily infection is a meme. Memes are good at the art of getting themselves copied from brain to brain or blog to blog. Memes do the same as genes except through different routes. Internet memes are altered deliberately through an act of creativity."[4]

It is the meme's close articulation with evolutionary genetics that makes it useful in understanding the revolutionary transfor-

A photograph uploaded to TwitPic by an Iranian blogger shows graffiti on a bus in Tehran reading, "Death to Khamenei." Ayatollah Ali Khamenei is Iran's ruling cleric. (*Source:* http://twitpic.com/c7afx)

mations that took place in culture in the course of the Iranian election crisis.

From Facebook walls to graffitied city walls, from billboards to circulating one-thousand rial bills[5] and city buses, the understanding was clear: "You are the media." To each individual was left the responsibility to counter the state's stranglehold on broadcasting. Social media may have been the site for the transmission of content, for the circulation of event announcements, articles, and commentary, but in the course of the uprising social media's amorphous networks of mimetic transmissions became the very blueprint for people's behavior, for their actions, and for their patterns of movement. Whether online or off, #iranelection transmitted packages of content with ease. Its network was alive. It was animated by living, breathing memes, each carrying units of cultural ideas and practice. As meme, each individual could in an

instant respond and retool any given prac-
tice or bend any habitual route towards its
revolutionary purpose: "if stopped u are
ONLY going shopping." Once at the bazaar,
these human viruses would spread, inviting
shopkeepers to join them, just as they had
invited the Revolutionary Guard, the riot police, and the security
forces, with slogans, flowers, and their gestures of kinship, to
come over to their side as they filled the boulevards and squares in
the early marches of the opposition (for video, scan QR code on
this page).[6]

Having themselves rewired into viral transmitters, everything,
any ordinary object the protestors touched, became a tool for the
resistance: green ink was used to write slogans or announce protest dates on circulating currency; a green screwdriver was used on
the job; the bus was reserved for the circulation of new slogans;
the green prayer rugs came to belong in Friday prayers; green ribbons and scarves were handpicked to adorn the city's statues. Virtually anything could be transformed into an object in solidarity
with the Green Movement. As replicating units of culture, the
days of the calendar too became objects of transformation. Target-
ing dates of historic significance to the regime, the opposition
infiltrated state-sponsored marches. In the course of these
marches, the effort was to "hack and redirect" the slogans and
symbols of the Islamic Republic.[7]

Thus, on July 21, 2009, almost exactly a month after the death
of Neda Agha-Soltan, protestors took to the streets to mark the
anniversary of the 30 Tir massacres.

In 1952, the thirtieth of the Persian month of Tir witnessed the
third and most massive day of consecutive protests following
Mohammad Mossadegh's surprising resignation as the prime

QR Protestors offer flowers to security forces in Kerman, Iran. (Video, June 16, 2009)
http://www.sup.org/mottahedeh/113/

minister of Iran. Mossadegh had in 1951 nationalized the oil industry to the chagrin of the Anglo-Iranian Oil Company (now known as BP). The British had taken their complaint before the international court at The Hague. Mossadegh himself was forced to travel to The Hague to argue in defense of nationalization, and had in the meeting emphasized that there was no precedent for the kind of judgment the court was being asked to render regarding the nationalization of oil. Further, he asserted, he could not put the nation "in the dangerous situation that might arise out of the court's decision." Having returned to Iran, Mossadegh asked for an audience with Mohammad Reza Shah. During his three-hour meeting with the monarch, he requested permission, as the Shah's prime minister, to take control of the armed forces in order to defend the nation against possible foreign invasion. The Shah rejected Mossadegh's request. Thus denied a right granted the prime minister by the Iranian constitution and the trust of the Shah to serve as the nation's minister of defense, Mossadegh had resigned.

The Shah appointed Ahmad Qavam (also known as Qavam Saltaneh) as his prime minister in Mossadegh's place. Qavam took office immediately and announced in a public communiqué that the days of defiance had come to an end and that the time for the obedience of the people to the will of the government had arrived. Reversing Mossadegh's nationalization policy, Qavam set out to resume negotiations with the British.

Enraged, members of the National Front, who were longtime supporters of Mossadegh, along with members of the Tudeh Communist Party, who were staunchly against Qavam's Western backing, poured into the street. Students, teachers, and many of the merchants of the bazaars joined the hundreds of protests around the country. The armed forces fired at the assembled crowds, killing many. Soon, though, regretting the bloodshed, military commanders called for a ceasefire. From their ranks, some joined the protestors. In witnessing the people's support for Mossadegh, the Shah rescinded his appointment of Qavam. Qavam resigned and the Shah reappointed Mossadegh prime minister and Iran's minister of defense.[8]

PLUG IN

Commemorating the day in 1952 on which the Iranian armed forces ultimately refused to turn their weapons on the people, the Iranian opposition took to the streets on 30 Tir, 2009, commencing another day of protests. According to *Time* magazine, "the government shut down mobile networks," well aware of the importance of 30 Tir for the opposition. The internet was also down for several hours. "But," *Time* wrote with some surprise, "protests appear to be coordinated and to be taking other forms apart from street action: on Tuesday, for example, thousands of disgruntled Tehranis tried to bring down the electrical grid at 9 P.M. by simultaneously turning on household appliances like irons, water heaters and toasters."[9] Using high-voltage appliances to generate a blackout, the protests continued without risking any more arrests.[10]

On Twitter, #iranelection was brimming with research on the most powerful high-voltage household utilities. That night, a

۳۰ تیر، اخبار ساعت ۹

Flash-mob campaign poster: "Plug in" #30Tir. (*Source:* http://www.dreamlandblog.com/2009/07/21/#002625)

stream of tweets enumerated quotidian engagements, to the puzzlement of many: "I am heating up food in the microwave." "I have the washing machine running." "I am ironing clothes tonight." "Blow-drying my hair." Iranian state television protected itself against the effects of the high-voltage protest by going to black before the nine o'clock news. This preemptive measure was thought to conceal the possible blackout the high-voltage campaign might generate. The Swiss-based Iranian blogger Omid Habibinia tweeted on the night of the "plug-in" campaign that he had received reports of blackouts in some parts of Tehran, Karaj, and Qazvin.[11] This was no minor victory. Rumors had been circulating both nationally and globally that the protests were isolated and that the opposition's campaigns were basically the shenanigans of some upper-class, West-identified Tehrani city dwellers. From the dark pockets of the night sky around the country, the plug-in campaign signaled otherwise.

The dozens of flash mobs and mass campaigns that emerged in the networked context of the Iranian election crisis, including the first high-voltage "plug-in" campaign that aimed to short-circuit Ahmadinejad's postelection television appearance; the campaign to "call the police at 4 PM about protests where there are none"; the "lights-on" protests in cars in all urban areas[12]; the flash-mob outings in cars on the road to the Caspian[13]; "the Green skies campaign" in which protestors released green balloons from the rooftops along with photos of those who had died during protests; and a "text the regime" campaign that encouraged protestors around the globe to send fiery text messages to government hackers who were attacking tweeps[14]—these constantly recalibrating memes virally transformed the ordinary and everyday into material for the resistance. The aim was to redirect the quotidian itself.

The deliberate and living memes of #iranelection underscore what Walter Benjamin intimated in his writings on childhood and the mimetic faculty, that the revolutionary consciousness is in fact a child's consciousness: playful, and in play mimetic and transformational. These acts of mimetic improvisation, of perception and in-the-moment transformation, acts that are made possible by web 2.0 technologies and social media, are the map from which the contemporary, flexible, and disorderly formations of protest and revolution gain in character. Not surprising, then, was the commonly held, rather playful notion that the Supreme Leader Ayatollah Khamenei, who frequently tweets, had at the first ritual Friday prayers after the election ordered Iranians to stage no further protests. He had warned the nation in the same breath, "I am following you all on Twitter."[15]

GOOGLE YOUTUBE

The winding roads leading to the Caspian Sea, the cloudless skies above the cities' rooftops and satellite dishes, the days of the calendar and their many commemorative ceremonies: these were not the only objects that were being virally infected and redirected during the course of the Iranian election crisis. Rooted in 2.0 technologies, #iranelection's gestures of resistance affected the entire online ecology of social networks as well. As one observer, Rahaf Harfoush, astutely noted in the midst of the crisis: "It's no longer about USERS leveraging a site's features, but organizational decisions which are adding a new variable to social media's role in impacting global change. For the first time, tech companies like Twitter, Facebook & Google are taking direct action in response to an unfolding crisis and are having a big impact."[16]

Critically aware of the paucity of information available to foreign journalists, the US State Department realized the significance of content mined from posts on Facebook and Twitter. "It is a very good example of where technology is helping," a senior official reported. "There are lots of people here watching." "There are some interesting messages going up."[17] The US government was

One million people voted online for Google to change its Google Doodle on June 21, 2009, in support of #iranelection. (*Source:* http://www.examiner.com/article/vote-for-google-logo-for-iran)

eager to ensure that it would continue to receive timely information as the protests continued. The State Department therefore asked Twitter to reschedule its maintenance in order to keep the service available as the situation on the ground unfolded.

On June 18, 2009, a mere six days after the election, Facebook added a test version of Persian to the site to ease the communication of content during the protests in Iran. In the press release announcing its addition of Persian, Facebook acknowledged the transformative effect that the aftermath of the elections had had on the platform:

> Since the Iranian election last week, people around the world have increasingly been sharing news and information on Facebook about the results and its aftermath. Much of the content created and shared on Facebook related to these events has been in Persian—the native language of Iran—but the users have had to navigate the site in English or other languages.
>
> Today we're making the entire site available in a test version of Persian, so Persian speakers inside of Iran and around the world can begin using it in their native language. Persian was already in translation before worldwide attention turned to the Iranian elections, but because of the sudden increase in activity we decided to launch it sooner than planned. This means that the translation isn't perfect, but we felt it was important to help more people communicate rather than wait.[18]

Google made a similar decision, announcing on June 18, 2009:

> We feel that launching Persian is particularly important now, given
> ongoing events in Iran. Like YouTube and other services, Google
> Translate is one more tool that Persian speakers can use to communi-
> cate directly to the world, and vice versa—increasing everyone's access
> to information. . . . The web provides many new channels of commu-
> nication that enable us to see events unfold in real-time around the
> world. We hope that Google Translate helps make all that information
> accessible to you—no matter what language you speak. We invite you
> to click on the "contribute a better translation" link and we'll learn
> from your correction.[19]

For many who tweeted with the hashtag #iranelection, Google
Translate eased the communication divide, enabling users access
to tweets and blogs throughout the crisis.[20] Keenly aware of
Google's unambiguous support less than one week into the crisis,
over one million people voted to change Google's logo for a day in
honor of #iranelection protestors.[21]

By aligning with protestors' active use of social media platforms, corporate adjustments to the solidarity of #iranelection
created real shifts in the ecology of online life. This affected the
deep architecture of journalism as well. YouTube removed its content restrictions, allowing the streaming of videos from the crisis

Tweet from @YouTube on June 19, 2009.

on the ground in Iran. On June 19, 2009, YouTube tweeted for the first time that CNN was streaming #iranelection videos live from its platform. That move was fortuitous.

LOADING ▮▮▮▮▯▯▯▯

The video of Neda Agha-Soltan's graphic death, posted first on Facebook on June 20, 2009, and then on YouTube, was destined for CNN two days later. "The clip was short, only forty seconds long," Setareh Sabety writes:

> We see a girl holding her chest and being helped to the ground by two men, one on each side. She is wearing blue jeans and a dark roosari (head scarf) and a tight, dark ropoosh (a long jacket worn by women in Iran in order to comply with the rules of hejab or Islamic covering). The two men are wearing blue jeans and short-sleeved shirts. One man has white pony-tailed hair, and the other is much younger with dark black hair. They help her down as we hear the voiceover of men speaking; we can hear one saying, "Abjee (sister) abjee—bring a car to take this one." We see a pool of blood gather under the girl's head. One of the men helping her keeps saying, "Neda joon natars. Neda natars (Neda dear don't be afraid. Neda don't be afraid)." Another man is heard saying, "Put pressure on it." The two men who helped her to the ground are trying to stop her bleeding, and a third has now approached and wants to help. We then hear the horrified screams of one of the men, "Vay, vaaaay." The companion with the white pony-tailed hair, whom we later learn was her music teacher, is now saying, "Neda, stay, Neda stay, Neda don't go." Blood starts coming out of her mouth and nose, making red, almost symmetric paths crossing her beautiful face and forming a pool under her head. The camera moves forward to a shot that shows six hands on her trying to stop the bleeding and one man kneeling in front of her rather helplessly. All this time, we hear "Neda stay, Neda don't go, Neda open, Neda open." Someone else says, "Open her mouth"; she turns to one side unconscious and her eyes roll back. We then hear the man who knew her name shout in a

shrill and most disturbing scream, "Dayoos haaaa, dayoos haa!" At that point, we know that she has taken her last breath. We hear screams. The clip ends as abruptly as it began.[22]

Neda was lauded as one of the top ten heroes of 2009 by *Time* magazine; the name Neda retrieved more than six thousand entries on Google's Persian-language site the day after the video of her death was uploaded on Facebook.[23] Her end, accompanied by the trending hashtag #Neda on Twitter, was described as "probably the most widely witnessed death in human history."[24] For many, such as the medical doctor Arash Hejazi who was present at the scene and who was responsible for uploading the Neda video, the digital record of her death was seen as a real weapon, one that confronted the Islamic Republic with evidence of its own corruption. The state's violence against its own people made the Islamic Republic's claim of being the ethical hub of Islam today null and void. As Hajatoleslam Mohammad Motahhari[25] noted: "Defending an Islamic regime by implementing non-Islamic and inhumane methods is as effective as trying to preserve the words and deeds of the Holy Prophet Mohammad through drinking alcohol. . . . Is that an example of the almost absolute freedom spoken of by the president in answer to a foreign journalist's question some time ago?"[26] "We died forty days ago / Bearing witness, / To the uncensored / 'Graphic content' / Of human cruelty!" writes Setareh Sabety in a poem honoring Neda.[27] The world did indeed bear witness to the repression and violence of the theocracy.[28] Recognizing the efficacy of social media in the transmission and circulation of that critical content, US president Barack Obama echoed, "No iron fist is strong enough to shut off the world from bearing witness."[29]

Retweeted and reposted on Facebook, Sabety's poem was among the hundreds of songs and videos that were dedicated to Neda and, through Neda's death mask, to the struggle of the Iranian people for rights and liberties denied them by the Islamic Republic. U2 dedicated its 2009 tour to the Iranian people, projecting images of the unrest alongside images from Shirin Neshat's photographic series *Women of Allah*. These photographs appeared on greened screens in every city as U2 opened their tour with their classic condemnation of bloodshed in the song "Sunday Bloody Sunday." Jon Bon Jovi was similarly moved, making a studio recording of the Ben E. King classic "Stand by Me" in Persian and English with the Iranian superstar Andranik (Andy) Madadian.[30] From her kitchen, on her signature solo guitar, Joan Baez made a YouTube recording of "We Shall Overcome" in honor of #iranelection, adding Persian lyrics that declared the people's ultimate victory.[31] Madonna too joined "the campaign for a free Iran" by dedicating her July 4 and 5 concerts to the people's struggle in Iran and by incorporating images of the uprising and the corollary violence in the montage to her music video "Rise Up, Now Is the Time." The video juxtaposed portraits of the Supreme Leader Ayatollah Khamenei and Iranian president Mahmoud Ahmadinejad and images of infamous African and North Korean dictators, an equation whose pointed condemnation of the current Iranian regime was hard to miss.[32] Little wonder then that Barack Obama would accept the Nobel Prize in the name of Neda, that "young woman who marches silently in the streets on behalf of her right to be heard even in the face of beatings and bullets."[33]

The video of Neda's death spurred a plethora of other responses too. The city of Rome renamed a street in her honor.[34] The Pirate Bay changed its color coding to green and renamed itself "The Persian Bay." The website Neda Speaks was immediately established as a platform for creative projects. The band The Airborne Toxic Event (TATE) supported Neda Speaks's efforts by holding a concert in honor of Neda and fashioning a music video, which with full creative license narrated the postelection crisis in hand-drawn images. Neda Speaks also initiated what later became a popular form of activism, namely, to take a stand for human rights by posting a selfie with the words "I am Neda" written on a blank sheet of paper. The campaign claimed that those who did this would be joining Iranians who were climbing onto their rooftops to call out Neda's name into the dark of night.[35] The proceeds from the Neda Speaks project were earmarked for Amnesty International, which has been working tirelessly for the release of several journalists, union organizers, graphic artists, and women's rights activists from Iran's prisons.

NedaNet.org, which was set up two days after Neda's death by a global network of hackers to provide routing services that would allow netizens to bypass Iranian surveillance during the postelection crisis, cooperated with anonymous hackers in Iran to enable communication and coordination. A Canadian collective of artists and musicians created the "We Are Neda" webnode dedicated to the liberties and freedoms that had been denied Neda and her fellow citizens. The collective also produced a music video that in four languages (English, Persian, French, and Spanish) reproduced a textual montage enumerating human rights and liberties.[36]

Neda memed at the "United for Iran" global campaign in Paris. "*Ma Hame Yek Nedaeem, Ma Hame Yek Sedaeem*" (We are all one Neda. We are all one calling). (© Reza Deghati)

The viral images of Neda's death were reproduced in so many thousands of formats, fora, and digital figures that any attempt to enumerate and preserve them would prove deficient. Perhaps, though, the most articulate representation of the memes generated by the video of Neda's death was the campaign "United for Iran" in Paris on July 25, 2009, where an estimated eight thousand protestors gathered around the Eiffel Tower to unfurl a two-kilometer-long banner with signatures of support and solidarity from all over the world.[37] Auxiliary events were held in one hundred and ten cities and six continents with over fifty thousand participants in all.

The most stunning of the images that circulated on #iranelection from the United for Iran global campaign were those from the grounds of the Eiffel Tower, where supporters all posed with masks of Neda, multiplying her image meme-like into a sea of thousands, a living, sensing networked body standing in an elsewhere, geo-tagged as Iran, where on the streets of Tehran Neda's life had been snuffed out.[38]

By a month into the Iranian election crisis, it was clear that the camera phone had become the eyes and ears of the globe, its recorded and collective act of witnessing. Retweeted, retooled, and repeatedly streamed, the digital camera's critical gesture of seeing formed the scrutinizing gaze of a collective sensorium.

COUNTRY: WORLDWIDE

In an essay on aesthetic and digital engagements with the video of Neda's death, Mazyar Lotfalian argues "that in order to understand the politicized images that emerged during Iran's presidential election in 2009, we need a theory of practice in the age of digital culture."[39] This suggests that contemporary theories of representation, indeed analyses engaged in traditional representational studies or even derived from communication and new media studies, "are insufficient to address the impact of digital culture" on #iranelection art and its effect on the public sphere.[40] The efficacy of this art, Lotfalian argues, derives from its mode of production, a convergence mode which also systematically eludes simplistic conclusions about the political effects, that is liberatory, alternative, residual, or otherwise, of the various mobile technologies used by the opposition. For as Minoo Moallem also notes, "the we-ness" that is constitutive of revolutionary Iran has forged a subject that "is not the sole author of its own text or the related modes of representation, since these modes of representations are formed by an endless chain of messages that are always subject to interpretation."[41] Thus, just as the reasons for the mimetic reproduction and the circulation of certain #iranelection images are historically grounded, Lotfalian argues, "their signification and usage are connected to historically-situated social practices."[42] Indeed, images culled from the protest culture of the Iranian Revolution are aestheticized forms of political expression drawing on a longer cultural history to give character to the art and images of #iranelection.

The most prominent cultural discourse underwriting the field of political graphic art during the Iranian Revolution was the Shi'ih theme of Karbala. The cultural and visual themes that are associated with the history of Karbala immediately differentiate the Shi'ih and Sunni branches of Islam. Too, they profile the profound significance rendered to Imam Hussein in Twelver Shi'ism.

Imam Hussein is known to the Muslim world as the grandson of the Prophet Muhammad, whose right to the leadership of the Muslim community was usurped by the caliphate. In the famous battle of Karbala in 680 CE, Imam Hussein was the principal victim of a ten-day carnage unleashed on the Prophet's family by the Umayyad Caliph Yazid. Although Imam Hussein was ultimately defeated in the course of this battle, he is revered by Iranian Shi'ihs as the one who stalwartly rose up against the enemy of Islam. On the tenth day of the month of Muharram, known as Ashura, the Caliph Yazid's considerable army brutally crushed Imam Hussein's rather small contingent, killed and beheaded the Imam, and proceeded to round up the women and children in his company. Captives of Yazid, the women and children were paraded in defeat to the capital at Damascus behind the head of their beloved Imam, which was lodged on a spear. Imam Hussein's death at Karbala and the subsequent events are viewed as a defining moment in collective Shi'ih memory. In more recent years, the battle of Karbala has been reinterpreted as an occasion for mourning and sermons of resistance. The Karbala allegory works, Lotfalian notes, "as a meta-discourse of right and wrong and calls the believers to rise up and fight injustices in the contemporary context."[43]

Effective as an oppositional narrative, the Karbala allegory was used in revolutionary posters and in cassette-tape sermons to mobilize the people against the Pahlavi monarchy: "At the time of the revolution, activists used the allegory of Karbala to liken the shah to Yazid, who committed horrendous injustices. Allegorical references to the martyrdom of Imam Hossein were central to the political aesthetics."[44] These became part of a "pedagogy of resistance," providing "space for various groups to articulate their dissatisfaction with the regime in different levels of language."[45] Since the establishment of the Islamic Republic, the state has been invested in maintaining hegemonic control over this particular cultural grammar. But the adaptation of this mainly textual, aural, and graphic history into other media, like all memes, has generated infinite citations and transformations in the digital environment.

Reza Deghati's 2009 video "Neda of Ashura" is among the most compelling of these viral rearticulations of the Karbala narrative (for video, scan QR code on this page).[46]

Drawing on the Revolution's graphic inscriptions of the scene of Ashura, Deghati inserts Neda's image on the Karbala landscape. She appears, in certain shots of the video, next to her slaughtered fellow martyrs. Memed and multiplied, she stands as witness, alongside Imam Hussein, to the mutilation of the nation at the hands of the riot police, the *basij* and the Revolutionary Guard. In other shots still, she is recognizable as a meme coded into the viral

QR Reza Deghati, Neda of Ashura. (Video, 2009) http://www.sup.org/mottahedeh/II19/

images that were circulating in social media during the early days of the 2009 crisis and that are embedded within the graphics of the video itself (see for example the photo on page 29). In the citation, permutation, and circulation of Neda as meme, the video's mimetics virally redirect the meanings and messages of the Karbala metadiscourse. Hacked in this way, the Karbala discourse too now bears witness. In Deghati's "Neda of Ashura," the most sacred allegory of Iranian Shi'ism comes to stand in the present as a witness to the violence of a state that claims the legacy of the Imams as its own.

This direct challenge to the Islamic state's rights to the Karbala allegory was cited and memed on the streets in the infectious retransmission of the Shi'ih call of "*Ya Hussein!*" which in ritual ceremonies of mourning summons the martyred Imam Hussein to take his legitimate place of honor in religious history. In the course of the 2009 protests, this commemorative cry was linked to Mir-Hossein Mousavi. A rhythmic viral slogan, "*Ya Hussein! Mir Hussein!*" emerged on the streets, which by tethering Mousavi's first name to Imam Hussein's, grafted Mousavi's legacy to the Imam's in the political history of antistate rebellion that is Shi'ism otherwise. Imam Hussein himself had thus been memed.

ADVANCED SETTINGS

On June 20, 2009, @persiankiwi tweeted the following:

> We have no future - no life - no hope - without you Allah - our creator - our leader #Iranelection Enna Allah va Analieh Rajeoon 8:30 PM - 20 Jun 2009[47]

As if placing a telephone call to God, @persiankiwi's tweeted evening prayer was transmitted to the hundreds of thousands of followers that were eagerly anticipating the next move of the Iranian opposition. @persiankiwi's tweet to the beyond, was in many respects reminiscent of a famous telephone call placed on behalf of Iran by Ayatollah Kafi.

In a widely distributed cassette recording of his 1978 sermon, Ayatollah Kafi is heard crying out to Imam Hussein to quit the plains of Karbala because the greater enemy is in Iran in the person of the Shah. This revolutionary call was reproduced on cassette tapes, multiplied, and circulated everywhere. His call to the Imam could be heard coming from cassette decks that were carried around on crowded sidewalks in every major city in Iran above the sound of bustling traffic. In response to the mechanical echoes of this revolutionary cry, the people of the Imam rose up to topple the Shah. In March 1979 the Islamic Republic of Iran was born as a Shi'ih nation as a consequence of this, "the cassette revolution."

In looking back on the history of the Iranian Revolution and the efficacy of Kafi's mediated and much circulated sermon, it becomes evident that Iranian Shi'ism is animated by an expectant messianism deeply rooted in its imamology. According to Twelver Shi'ism, the Prophet Muhammad, his daughter Fatima, and the twelve Imams compose the luminous body of Muhammad's revelation, whose role is to cast a guiding light into the depths of the divine teachings for the followers of Muhammad over time. The martyred Third Imam, Imam Hussein, stands as the heroic figure of Iranian Islam, called upon to participate in historical happenings as a figure of personal transformation and political revolution. His return alongside the Twelfth Imam is projected as Judgment Day.

A mystery surrounds the whereabouts of the Twelfth Imam, however. This mystery advances his significance for Shi'ih history. As a young child (in 873 CE), the Twelfth Imam went into occultation and has for hundreds of years resided on the Green Island. The Green Island is a timeless place, a land of no-where (Na-koja-Abad), a land without coordinates. His imminent return, messianic in conception, imbues every moment of time with significance. "Present simultaneously in the past and the future," writes Henri Corbin of the Twelfth Imam, the Hidden Imam "has been for ten centuries the history itself of Shi'ite consciousness, a history over which, of course, historical criticism loses its rights, for its events, although real, nevertheless do not have the reality of events in our climates." Though he is hidden from sense perception, it is thought that the Twelfth Imam exists in the hearts of his followers and is the "mystical pole" (*qotb*) on which the existence of the world depends. The no-where in which the Twelfth Imam resides, along with the other Imams, is self-sufficient, immune, and closed to the material world, at least according to the accounts of those who have seen it. Only those who are summoned are able to find their way to this unknown region—to an imaginal world that is described as both an oasis in the desert and an island in green waters. The space of the imaginal, advanced as the realm of the dead, is, Jonathan Sterne reflects, "as extensive as the storage and transmission capabilities" of the culture itself.[48]

The Iranian Revolution was the first attempt at the viral transmission of the realm of the imaginal. By all accounts it was this utopian world that the Islamic theocracy attempted to establish in the sensory world as the body of the isolationist nation it named the Islamic Republic of Iran. Self-sufficient and immune to all outside contaminants, the imaginal world would be manifested by the nation's sensorium as the body of the Iranian nation itself. For as Kafi's telephone call suggested, this imaginal world is present both in the past and in the future. His ritual call enacted the history of Islam and its redeemed messianic future simultaneously on a utopian plane that belongs to no time and no place (Na-koja-Abad). The telephone call mimetically transferred that plane into this material one, virally copying its spatiotemporal coordinates into a present that also bears the marks of a utopian future. Constituted by the empirical body of the believers, this historical stage is the national body alive in the present as it becomes, in the course of that significant ritual transmission, the future purified setting for the Iranian nation itself.

The 2009 vote for the president of the Islamic Republic was clearly signposted by the opposition as one such uncompromising ritual of transmission. Five days after the announcement of the election results, @persiankiwi tweeted, "chanting 'my brother - my martyr - I

Dressed in Imam Hussein's costume for the Ta'ziyeh mourning play, a protestor holds a sign that reads, "My martyred brother, I will reclaim your vote." (*Photo:* L'Anonyme, Tehran, 2009. *Source:* http://creativetimereports.org/2013/06/12/fitna-iranian-elections/)

will claim your vote for you!' - #Iranelection 2:07 PM - 17 Jun 2009," as if his very transmission would redeem history for all time.

In the heat of the summer and in the midst of the protesting crowds, a young man dressed in the outfit ritually assigned to Imam Hussein in Muharram mourning ceremonies, Ashura graphics, and the Shi'ih passion play (the *ta'ziyeh*) held a sign: "My martyred brother, I'll take back your vote."[49] Captured on a digital camera and uploaded by a user, the image of the young man dressed as a role-carrier for Imam Hussein and the messianic and youthful Twelfth Imam, both, was transmitted to CNN's *iReport* platform within hours. What Benjamin once said about the early telephone is true of the messianic (and revolutionary) transformations that were taking place on social media as a result of #iranelection: "The voice that slumbered in those instruments was a newborn voice."[50]

"The telephone has always been inhabited with the rhetoric of the departed,"[51] writes Avital Ronell. That digital technologies are employed to establish contact with those in the imaginal realm, such as the youthful Twelfth Imam, implies that "contact with the Other has been disrupted; but it also means that the break is never absolute. Being on the telephone will come to mean, therefore, that contact is never constant nor is the break clean." Kafi's text is telephonically charged in the call summoning Imam Hussein to claim his rightful place in history, but so is the printed message of the young man donned in Imam Hussein's gear promising to set history aright on CNN's *iReport*. The viral transmission of his youthful figure, which also signals the presence of the Twelfth Imam on all #iranelection platforms, evidences the mimetic presence of the imaginal world in the empirical world. Contact has been established. Today is Judgment Day.

"ALLAH-O-AKBAR"

"Rooftops are no longer places where you plant your satellite dishes or line-dry your clothes," writes Homa Maddah. Instead, the rooftop is a place "where you shout out all that you have kept inside in these years within the confines of your four-walls. On the rooftop, the city is my four-walls. . . . And allah o akbar is no longer a religious slogan in a different language but the cry of protest when no other cry is possible. It stands for justice."[52]

The call "*Allah-o-akbar! Khomeini rahbar!*" (God is Great! Khomeini is the guide!) was one of the slogans of the Iranian Revolution, chanted nightly from rooftops in cities across the country by protestors defying curfew to call an end to the monarchy. The chant "merged a cosmological invocation and a political project," writes Setrag Manoukian. "On the one hand, the idea of a 'guide' referenced the messianic dimension of Shiism. Invoking God, the chant called for the return of a rightful guide for the community after the occultation of the last Imam, the descendant of the Prophet who was endowed with a reflection of Muhammad's light."[53] On the other hand, "the call for Khomeini to be leader was a clear disavowal of the Pahlavi monarchy."[54] "Shouting and screaming at a given time of the night—a protest in which everyone participated—broke the silence imposed by military rule." During the course of the Iranian Revolution, the "Tehran night soon became a site of protest and revolt. The roof (*bam*, or *pohst-ebam*) found a new function as a liminal urban space, neither public nor private. . . . The massive participation of voices, some of which were broadcast live and others carried through electronic relay, created a community of protest."[55]

The nightly cries of "*Allah-o-akbar!*" from rooftops reemerged in the summer of 2009. On June 20, 2009, @persiankiwi tweeted:

> http://bit.ly/WXYu3 - Tehran is alive with the Sea of Green - #Iranelection - RT RT RT 12:12 AM - 20 Jun 2009

Referring to the sea of people on the streets of Tehran donning iridescent green in opposition to the regime, @persiankiwi transmitted to his followers the hashtag #iranelection as their slogan and embedded in his tweet a bitly-shortened link that led  to a YouTube video posted by oldouz84. On that site an anonymous poet had recorded a video, inscribing in her verses the calendrical "day of destiny," a day that marks the imminent arrival of the Day of Judgment.

During Friday prayers on June 19, 2009, the Supreme Leader had reiterated his support for Ahmadinejad's presidency, declaring a halt to the protests and promising their active suppression. This was a promise, not a threat. The people's refusal to stop the protests would inevitably usher in an epic confrontation between the forces of good and the forces of evil.[56] Indeed, the next day, June 20, 2009, witnessed the death of many, including Neda Agha-Soltan, on the streets at the hands of the militia and the Iranian security forces.

The YouTube video that @persiankiwi linked to in the tweet opens to a dark screen, and the poet's voice narrates in Persian from outside the frame: "Friday 29 Khordad 1388 [June 19, 2009].

QR *Where is this place? This is Iran. My Land and yours.* (Video, June 19, 2009) http://www.sup.org/mottahedeh/1126/

Tomorrow is Saturday. Tomorrow is the day of destiny" (for video, scan QR code on preceding page).

> Tonight, the sound of Allah-o-akbar can be heard louder and louder than previous nights
> Where is this place?
> Where is this place where everything has been closed down?
> Where is this place where the only thing people can do is shout the name of God?
> Where is this place where the sound of Allah-o-akbar can be heard louder and louder?
> Every day I wait to see if at night the voices will be louder and louder
> My body trembles [*short pause*] I do not know if God trembles too
> Where is this place where we have been innocently imprisoned?
> Where is this place where no one remembers us?
> Where is this place, where our voices are heard worldwide through our silence? [*gentle sobbing*]
> Where is this place [*sobbing*] where the blood of its young people is shed and people stand on the street and pray over their blood?
> On that same blood they pray
> Where is this place where its people are named "lowlifes and thugs"?
> Where is this place?
> Do you want me to tell you?
> This is Iran.
> This is my land and yours [*pause*]
> This is Iran.[57]

To encode that Saturday as the Day of Judgment was to promise the messianic confrontation of Imam Hussein with the brute force of evil, personified within the Karbala narrative by the figure of Caliph Yazid. In popular dramas or Karbala mourning plays, Judgment Day also always marks the messianic return of the youthful occulted Twelfth Imam, redeeming in this one moment of mystical innocence, courage, and heroism the history of all time for all time.

"Varying in pitch, timbre, loudness, and duration, at times the chants respond to one another, at others they vanish into the darkness. While dispersed, they sustain the stillness of the image and turn darkness into a narrative."[58] In calling on the greatness of God, the persistent loudness of the people's voice makes the poet's body tremble. In this transmission of a collective voice that is heard worldwide, she wonders if the people's call is received: "I do not know if God trembles too," she whispers. As Manoukian observes, "By establishing a link between collective action and individual sensation, the video constitutes Iran as a specific place."[59] The poet's sobbing voice as the symptom of a trembling body programs her. Like the multiplying memes of Neda in Deghati's video, she is a mourner who witnesses the tragedy of the nation in the here and now. Gesturing towards recognized ritual mournings for Ashura, the video encodes this moment as the there and then of Karbala, indeed meming that brutal mutilation of Imam Hussein and his party as the mutilation of the protestors in the here and now of the present. This is, as Manoukian puts it, "perilous communication."[60] In the Rooftop Poet's video, Iran is Karbala memed.

The Rooftop Poet's nightly YouTube messages continued, now as communiqués to God. Following a day of brutal state violence against the protesting crowds, the poet sobs into the video that night, sometimes amplifying the voices that seem to  multiply and gain in intensity in calling upon God (for video, scan QR code on this page):

20 Khordad 1388 [June 20, 2009], Saturday
God, last night we all called you so much
We all cried for you so much

. . . .

The sound is really louder tonight, [*pause*] much louder [*loud sobbing*]
Why were you asleep?
Why can your voice not be heard?
Why don't you show any reaction?

QR *O God! Listen carefully! If you are asleep, wake up! They are calling you!*
(Video, June 20, 2009) http://www.sup.org/mottahedeh/1128/

We have put our lives in the palms of our hands
Why don't you [*inaudible*] show yourself?

. . . .

Listen This voice is ours Allah-o-akbar [*louder*]
A voice that has no other outlet Allah-o-akbar, Allah-o-akbar
Listen Allah-o-akbar
This [voice is coming out of our depths]
Allah-o-akbar [*from different direction*]
Allah-o-akbar
Why did you leave us so defenseless?
Allah-o-akbar [*children, more distant*]
Allah-o-akbar [*one man's voice*] Allah-o-akbar [*other voices*]
Allah-o-akbar [*several women's voices*]
Allah-o-akbar [*voiceover sighing*]
Allah-o-akbar
O God! Listen how they are calling you Listen, listen [*sobs*]
If you are asleep, wake up! It is not the time to sleep
You have to listen
Allah-o-akbar, Allah-o-akbar
Listen well
Listen, so there is no excuse for you when we meet in the afterlife
Allah-o-akbar
So you do not say, "I did not hear their voices"
Allah-o-akbar
Don't say that we did not call you, so you did not hear us
Listen well [*sob*]
[They] are all calling you
Listen well.[61]

Reflecting in one of her earlier recordings, the poet observed that *Allah-o-akbar* is "the simplest, first and best" of ways for people to call one another. "They can take away our SMS, our internet, and our mobile phones, but we will show that with the sounding of our Allah-o-akbar we can still gather together. People are calling God with their entire being," she reflected. Deprived of all media, people themselves had become transmitters that could organize, gather, call, and communicate. Pondering the utopian, she mused, "Perhaps . . . [the viral transmission of] . . . Allah-o-akbar can make the divine throne tremble" (*Allah-o-akbar arshe elahi ra be larze khahad avard*).

But by June 20 it was clear that a response from the divine realm was not forthcoming. Realizing that God has not shown himself in the playing field, the poet's video recording encodes a wake-up call to him. Preserving and transmitting a multiplicity of voices—the child, the women, the men, and now too the voices of the dead (Neda)—it is as if the poet has canned the voices she mediates.[62] Transporting herself through the fibers of the video to the threshold of the sacred, she insists, "Wake up!" "Listen!" She addresses God, "This voice is coming out of our depths."

From the dimly lit night over Tehran, the video is the carrier of voices, a tool that also preserves them. The YouTube video is, in this poet's narrative vision, fundamentally a vehicle that transmits an aggregate sensory chain that speaks directly to God and jolts him into the consciousness of the present state of emergency.

"No news aggregator tells of the ravaged city exhaling in the dusk, nor summons the defiant cries that rise into the night," writes *New York Times* journalist Roger Cohen of his mournful loss of access to the protests with the evacuation of the foreign press a week after the election. "No miracle of technology renders the lip-drying taste of fear. No algorithm captures the hush of dignity. . . . I confess that, out of Iran, I am bereft. A chunk of me is back in Tehran where I saw the Iranian people rise in the millions to reclaim their votes and protest the violation of their Constitution." Cohen's descriptive rush of being on the streets in the midst of the protesting crowds moves me deeply, but I tend to disagree with him on the material and emotional effects of aggregators and algorithms. For unaccustomed as we are to our own cybernetic existence, we tend not to notice the full sensory reality of a given tweet—an algorithm of sorts, as Cohen rightly points out. We brush it off flippantly; even in retrospect, how potent could a tweet that was once favorite and only thrice retweeted possibly be?

More than just 140 characters, @persiankiwi's tweet in which the Rooftop Poet's YouTube video was embedded was partly eyes and partly ears bearing witness on behalf of the globe to the swarming Sea of Green on the streets and boulevards of the city of Tehran. The tweet was also partly a connector to another realm, and a simulator too: by way of transmission it brought that realm into this material one. As a time machine, @persiankiwi's tweet recoded the past into the present, and forward into a utopian future "of the day of destiny" yet unseen. Technologically reconstituted and virally memed, the Rooftops Poet's voice in the video posted by @persiankiwi in this same tweet, along with the thousands of voices the poet herself encoded, turned the tweet into a sonorous alarm clock; it was an alarm clock designed at once to wake up God and to call in Judgment Day. The urgent wake-up call that the video transmitted was the voice of the Islamic cyborg, a collective voice born out of Khomeini's own postrevolutionary vision of technology. In that creative vision, a human body endowed with purified technological limbs, was promised, by the Imam himself, direct access to the realm of the sacred.

THE URFORM

June 16, 2009, saw a visionary tweet on #iranelection. @persiankiwi wrote:

> everybody try to film as much as poss today on mobiles - v\imptnt - these are eyes of world #Iranelection 8:08 AM - 16 Jun 2009

This tweet, which equated the digital camera of the mobile phone with the eyes of the world, in truth cyborgian in conception, situated technology as the mimetic body of the collective. While in many ways @persiankiwi's tweet repeated the revolutionary fusion of the body and technology in the anticolonial uprisings of the 1950s and 1960s, in which the radio itself became the ear of the receiver, his June 16 tweet was also crucially linked to the project of the Islamic Republic itself.

Recalling the practice of "airwave warfare" during the Algerian War of Independence, Frantz Fanon noted that the French were particularly "quick to pick up the wavelengths of the transmitters." Algerian programming, he writes,

> [was] then systematically jammed [*brouillés*], and the "Voice of Fighting Algeria" became inaudible. A new form of struggle was born. Leaflets counseled Algerians to keep tuned in for durations of two to three hours. In the course of one broadcast, a second station, transmitting over another wavelength would relay the first jammed station. The listener, thus incorporated into the battle of the airwaves, had to figure out the tactics of the enemy, and in a manner almost physical, muscular, outmaneuver the strategy of the adversary. Often, only the operator, his ear glued to the apparatus, would have the unanticipated chance to hear the Voice. The other Algerians present in the room received the echo of this voice through the device of a privileged interpreter, who, at the end of the broadcast, was literally besieged. Precise questions were then posed to this incarnated voice.[63]

In Fanon's description, John Mowitt observes,

> we are presented with the figure of the incarnated voice, not the word made flesh (at least not simply this), but the broadcast materialized in the receiver, that is the operator whose ear has fused with the apparatus. . . . Fanon goes on to transform the subjects who have incorporated themselves within the national conflict into radios. As he insists: "Every Algerian, for his part, broadcast and transmitted [émet et tramsmet] this new language," a formulation whose lexical details make it clear that the operator who earlier incarnated the "Voice" has now given way to a collective formation whose nearest conceptual analogue might be a disseminated network.[64]

In the context of the Algerian War, the new national body was articulated with the revolutionary voice of the radio. As one technologically enhanced body, the Algerian people cocreated a disseminated network, a collective sensorium, fortified to cast off the colonial yoke.

For Khomeini's Iran some years later, the recalibration of the collective's senses through media technologies promised both national sovereignty and otherworldly access. He articulated this move through an attempt to sanctify media in light of what he called the nation's "state of self-estrangement." Crucially, he attributed this state of estrangement to the national body's alienation from its own sense perceptions, in that these were configured by the senses' fundamental attachment to media—the eyes to the camera, the ears to sound technologies. The pollution of the national sensorium by globalizing forces working through media technologies implied, in other words, the pollution and the weakening of the national body and the distraction of the nation's energies away from production and national knowledge, away even from life. The Iranian Marxist and postcolonial thinker Jalal Al-e Ahmad had articulated this notion succinctly in the opening paragraph of his book *Occidentosis* as an experience akin to the attack of a tongue worm:

> I speak of being afflicted with "Westitis" the way I would speak of being afflicted with cholera. If this is not palpable let us say it is akin to being stricken by heat or cold. But it is not that either. It is something more on the order of being attacked by tongue worm. Have you ever seen how wheat rots? From within. In any case we are dealing with an illness, a disease imported from abroad, and developed in an environment receptive to it.[65]

Under the former Pahlavi rule, it was media technologies that were used to transport this poisonous disease to Iran. As such, Khomeini saw the estrangement of the nation from its senses as a direct response to the monarchic regime's submission of Iranian media to Western powers, and hence to the contamination of the national body by foreign pollutants. This take on technology was itself not new to Iranian Shi'ih thought. Other Shi'ih modernists such as Al-e Ahmad and Ali Shari'ati had attributed the "Westoxification" of the nation to contaminants introduced by Western technologies in the

1960s and 1970s. In Khomeini's discourse, however, this contamination did not add up to a complete rejection of media. Instead, such "features of modernity" were in need of a thorough cleansing. For Khomeini, the promise of sanctified mediating technologies was the purification and the consolidation of the collective itself.[66] The "rotting mass" would be regenerated by these means.

In the discourse of the new Islamic Republic, the state effort to sanctify technology aimed to provide the nation with its own sovereignty. Attached to the nation's collective senses, the purified technology would differentiate the subject's world from the rest of the globe. With the media as the collective senses of the nation, its state of sanctification would grant pure and direct access to an otherworldly realm, a no-place (Na-koja-Abad) where the prophets and all the Imams reside. In his philosophical works, Corbin called this the site of the original image, the realm of the imaginal, a no-where that is everywhere, a ubiquitous realm of pure sensory experience.[67]

The figure of an Islamic cyborg was forged in Khomeini's thought to access and transmit this precise realm. In going through technology, Iran's senses (the aesthesis), once regenerated, could be politicized in collective and revolutionary ways that were indeed capable of mimetically transmitting and reproducing that imaginal realm on the earthly plane. Forty years earlier, this capacity in film technology allowed Walter Benjamin to imagine "an alternative mode of aesthetics on par with modern, collective experience, an aesthetic that could counteract, at the level of sense perception, the political consequences of the failed—that is capitalist, imperialist, destructive and self-destructive—reception of technology."[68]

By 2009, Khomeini's utopian vision of the national body's relationship to purified media technologies had enacted a fundamental genetic mutation in the senses of the collective. The sensory network had been technologically altered over the course of the nation's thirty-year history to see collectively through the eyes of the purified lens of the camera and to hear by means of its aural media. This understanding of the materialization of media technologies in the body also implied, in its urform, a telephonic logic of transmission and contact with the messianic figures present in the expanses of the imaginal world. The viral possibilities of digital technologies, such as Twitter and YouTube, tethered to the mimetics of horizontal, many-to-many transmissions, merely amplified that logic of contact—a logic that had forwarded Ayatollah Kafi's telephone call to Imam Hussein on the plains of Karbala during the Iranian Revolution. In this viral tethering, the voice of the collective as a disseminated network would invite all, including God himself, to take part in the unfurling of a revolution that was scheduled for Judgment Day.

III SELFIE: Solidarity & everyday life

The meme-like character of the #iranelection protests was magnified when thousands of Twitter subscribers placed a green overlay on their avatars in solidarity with protestors on the ground. An independent innovator, Arik Fraimovich, was still developing the app for the green overlay for helpiranelection.com when one tweet on June 17, "Green your avatar in support of the folks in Iran," set things in motion. Overnight the campaign took on a life of its own. By a month into the crisis, 230,000 people had used the app to green their avatars in support of #iranelection. Eager to make their approach to the crisis relevant and responding actively to @persiankiwi's early request[1] in the midst of dangers facing his own team, many more changed their location to Tehran and set their time zone to +03:30 GMT. In this way, they aimed to protect the identities of tweeps who were posting critical content and updates from the protests in Iran. While the Rooftop Poet's video signaled a temporal meming, an atomism, in which the past was also the future-present, this gesture of solidarity with #iranelection on Twitter implied the geo-tagging of the entire globe as Tehran +03:30 GMT. Tehran was everywhere memed.

A pixelated collage of Neda Agha-Soltan was created from the greened Twitter avatars to reflect the reverberations of her death in the life of netizens on #iranelection. But the portrait itself was clearly based on a case of mistaken identities. The collage of the greened avatars was, in other words, a pixelated glitch. To trace the story of Neda's portrait and its life-threatening consequences, we must return to the threshold of mainstream media.

In the midst of the postelection crisis, an English professor at the University of Tehran, Neda Soltani, had received 367 friend requests on Facebook by journalists and bloggers from around the world. Having had no access to pictures from the life of the music student, Neda Agha-Soltan, after the circulation of the video of her death on YouTube, journalists had searched Facebook. One would assume that it was by some muddled process of elimination that they had identified Soltani as the murdered Neda Agha-Soltan. Journalists downloaded photos that Soltani had posted of herself on Facebook as her avatar and hastily attached them to the stories they were about to broadcast on a modern Iranian woman's street murder, a death captured by an "amateur video" and posted on social media.

Pixelated poster of Neda made with Twitter's greened avatars in support of #iranelection.
(*Source:* http://negarpontifiles.blogspot.com/2010/04/green-is-new-green.html)

Meanwhile, there had been several student arrests during a horrific government raid on June 14, 2009, leading to the death of five students and the resignation of 119 faculty members at Tehran University, where Soltani also taught. In solidarity, friends of those who had been injured, killed, or arrested at the university had coordinated sit-in protests late into the night. Though uninvolved and disinterested in the entire pitch of the postelection crisis, Soltani felt obliged, as a member of the university's board, to stay on while the students were on campus. She returned home late one night to find messages from family, friends, and colleagues, all wondering what had happened. She recalls the worry in their voices: "We saw you on CNN, we saw you on Fox News, we saw you on Farsi channels, Iranian channels. The international media was using a picture of me taken from my Facebook account to accompany the footage of Neda Agha-Soltan's death."[2]

Forty-eight hours after Neda's death, Soltani's tightly veiled portrait had gone viral. People all over the world reposted it on Twitter, Flickr, FriendFeed, and Facebook. They made posters of it and built beautifully lit memorials to it, sometimes placing it next to a still from the video of Neda's bloody death. While Neda's name became the voice of the resistance, it was Soltani's portrait that had, within hours, become the very face of the opposition, a living symbol of the uprising. "When I saw people all over the world demonstrating with my photo, putting up shrines, lighting candles—it was just like sitting there and watching my own funeral," she recalls. The impact of the critical blunder was far greater on her life.

Threatened by the attention that the digital video of Neda's death had brought on from abroad, the Iranian government was eager to wash its hands of the whole tragedy. The Iranian Ministry of Intelligence sent agents to Soltani's home. They interrogated her, pushing for a way to make the viral video appear as a piece of propaganda, indeed a staged documentary by the BBC's Persian channel for Facebook. Soltani refused to cooperate. "I remember one of the agents telling me: 'You as a single individual do not count for us—right now, the national security of our Islamic fatherland is in question.' I was so distressed and afraid. I simply couldn't believe a photo could ruin my whole life," she recalls. Accused of betraying her nation as an agent of the CIA, she was instructed to sign a written confession of her involvement in faking her death in the digital video of Neda. She realized that to do that would be her own death sentence.

Soltani made arrangements to leave the country overnight. In a matter of two weeks, the viral circulation of a Facebook photo had turned her life inside out. She went from being a professor of English literature in Tehran to an anxious asylum-seeker, waiting at a refugee camp in Germany. In the hands of Western media, her profile picture on Facebook had exposed her life to extreme danger, subject to accusations of a breach of national security in Iran.

SELECT & CROP

The digital video that captured the death of Neda Agha-Soltan memed political tensions on the other side of the Atlantic. The stakes this time were the national security of the United States. On June 23, 2009, three days after the Neda video went viral on social media, it was referenced during a press conference at the White House. President Barack Obama opened the proceedings by commenting on the situation in Iran, noting the courage and dignity of the Iranian people. Staying interference, Obama remarked on the extraordinary images that were being transmitted via social media: "Despite the Iranian government's efforts to expel journalists and isolate itself," he said,

> powerful images and poignant words have made their way to us through cell phones and computers, and so we've watched what the Iranian people are doing. This is what we've witnessed. We've seen the timeless dignity of tens of thousands of Iranians marching in silence. We've seen people of all ages risk everything to insist that their votes

are counted and that their voices are heard. Above all, we've seen courageous women stand up to the brutality and threats, and we've experienced the searing image of a woman bleeding to death on the streets. While this loss is raw and extraordinarily painful, we also know this: Those who stand up for justice are always on the right side of history.

Asked at the very end of the press conference whether he had seen the YouTube video of Neda's death, Obama affirmed that he had and underscored his own response to it. "Heartbreaking," he emphasized, adding, "I think that anybody who sees it knows that there's something fundamentally unjust about that. . . . I have concern about how peaceful demonstrators and people who want their votes counted may be stifled from expressing those concerns."[3]

Hearst columnist Helen Thomas, known as "the first lady of the press" and notorious for the blunt and confrontational questions she has posed in the White House Briefing Room to ten presidents of the United States, interrupted Obama at this point, recalling his recent decision to retract an earlier promise to disclose classified images from over two hundred criminal investigations of prisoner abuse. These images would serve to document the coercive measures taken by the Bush administration to interrogate detainees held by US authorities abroad in the aftermath of the 9/11 attacks. Interrupting Obama's train of thought, Thomas asked, "Then why won't you allow the photos ..." Obama understood. "Hold on a second, Helen," he insisted without a moment's hesitation, "That's a different question."

It was held that "the most direct consequence" of releasing the photographs of the prisoner abuse "would be to further inflame anti-American opinion" and to put American troops in danger.[4]

FILTER

Taken at Abu Ghraib by American soldiers stationed at the time in Iraq, the shattering images of prisoner abuse, leaked five years earlier, depicted Iraqi detainees stacked naked in piles and pyramids.

Some were chained to beds or placed in other painful or humiliating positions. Others, again, were clearly being tormented by dogs. During the presidency of George W. Bush, these crushing images had become signposts of the military occupation of Iraq, leading to anger and distrust in many areas of the Middle East. From the intensity of the rage that erupted over their circulation, one could gather that, above all, shame and honor were at stake. Indeed as one of the prisoners in the 2009 Iranian postelection crisis who had testified to being raped in prison admitted, breaking the silence around similar humiliations suffered in Iranian prisons was the equivalent of "committing a social suicide."[5]

In the summer of 2004, a government-sponsored public art series including two of the newly leaked Abu Ghraib images appeared on the soundproofed walls of Sadr freeway in Tehran. The first panel on the left was a painted reproduction of the infamous photograph

A public art project on city walls in Tehran depicting Abu Ghraib abuses. (*Photo:* Negar Mottahedeh)

of the uniformed Private First Class Lynndie England holding a leash tied to the neck of an Iraqi prisoner who was curled naked in a fetal position on an Abu Ghraib prison floor. This image sent shockwaves around the world, as did the one reproduced in the second panel of a hooded Iraqi prisoner balancing on a platform with electrical wires attached to his limbs and genitals.

Such haunting images of humiliating torture reinforced for many the admonitions of Colonel Mathieu in *The Battle of Algiers*, a film representing the Algerian anticolonial war that came back in vogue as a training film on guerrilla warfare during the Bush administration. The colonel's words impressed on audiences of the early 1960s, as they do even today, that the continued presence of an imperial military where it is not wanted requires of it to identify sources of populist agitation by any means necessary. An ordinary citizen's support of the occupation, whether in the name of liberation or progress, implies his or her tacit acceptance of all the repercussions of military force—anything and everything, including surveillance and torture.

Not unlike user-selected photo-filters native to social media platforms such as Instagram today, the painted images on the walls of the Sadr freeway bore the imprint of the hand that had transformed them from a soldier's souvenirs to magnified paintings for the public. This was striking, and striking too were the words written in Persian to one side of the second panel—"*Emrooz Araq*" (Today Iraq)—a caption like one that attempts to anchor an Instagram image in the quotidian: "Here's where I am." "This is what I saw." "This is Iraq today." Rendered in the third and fourth panels were the Shrine of Imam Ali in Najaf, Iraq, and the Dome of the Rock, Al-Quds, in Jerusalem. And imprinted there on the fourth was a quotation attributed to Imam Ali, who as the son-in-law of the Prophet Muhammad, called on the believer to be the enemy of tyranny and a supporter of the victims of injustice. Following a gap on the wall, a final panel on the Sadr wall depicted three soldiers in combat, on bended knee and surrounded by smoke and fire.

The last heavy combat Iranian soldiers saw was the vicious eight-year war between Iran and Iraq, in which Iran sacrificed the majority of its male labor force, men who would now be in their thirties, forties, or early fifties. Seen from the perspective of that war, the messages communicated in the fusion of these five panels seemed ambiguous at best. The images arrived as both the bearers of the latest news—"Today Iraq"—and a prescription for pious living: "Be a force against evil and a defender of the good." Made to "flit past the viewer under the pressure of the thumb,"[6] as did the pictures in those early little flip books, or swiped and "hearted" like Instagram images on a tiny screen, the panels bore the mark of the newest day, "the proper object of the journal."[7] Constellated in a confluence of the past-present, the images carried a reminder. They signaled a crucial moment for the devout and a moment of military defense, perhaps visual exhortation to an end open to question.

"Then why won't you allow the photos?"

The fifth of the six panels went up later that summer to fill the gap on the wall. It portrayed two men. One lay face down on a red carpet, and the other, sitting next to him, gazed out of the frame toward the sixth panel, the one depicting the three men engaged in military combat. The caption on the left side of the fifth panel completed the temporal atomism of the wall, mirroring the present-past gaze that would transport the viewer's look from the fifth panel to the sixth: "*Dirooz Felestin*" (Yesterday Palestine).

WRITE A CAPTION

There is little question about the messages contained in the viral images of women from the 2009 election crisis that were circulating online and then in mainstream news and print media. Appearing in enlarged photos enveloped by fine print were young women, beautifully decked out in states of half-unveil, sporting green ribbons and freshly tended, shiny manicures; groups of women in their twenties and thirties, arms raised high in gestures of assured victory, marching the streets of Tehran alongside their friends. And again, women in tight, thigh-length overcoats and colorful headscarves; or, adorning the front page of the *New York Times*, a lone middle-aged figure standing on a platform holding a close-up of a smiling Mousavi, as all around her men with digital devices attempt to take that one shot no one had grabbed of her fully veiled figure in the midst of the teaming crowds.

As Haleh Anvari notes, the veil is like "Iran's Eiffel Tower": "To Western visitors, it drop[s] a pin on their travel maps, where the bodies of Iranian women [become] a stand-in for the character of Iranian society. When I worked with foreign journalists for six years, I helped produce reports that were illustrated invariably with a woman in a black chador. I once asked a photojournalist why. He said, 'How else can we show where we are?'"[8] These images and their pointed captions, especially in mainstream media, speak to a burgeoning scuffle for change conceived in terms of an imagined secular democracy in which women appear in the public sphere relatively unfettered by a piece of black cloth.

"If you wish to see Iran as it is," writes Haleh Anvari, "you need go no further than Facebook and Instagram. Here, Iran is neither fully veiled nor longing to undress itself. Its complex variety is shown through the lens of its own people, in both private and public spaces."[9] The fantasy of the Oriental woman's liberation as a result of a much celebrated Western intervention or a recognizable revolution against an oppressive regime (however pointedly defined), though centuries in the making, goes little further than the printed page. It is perhaps for this very reason that the #IamMajid campaign at the six-month point of the #iranelection crisis received the kind of praise it did from the Nobel laureate and Iranian human rights lawyer Shirin Ebadi.

16AZAR

December 7, 2009, corresponding to the sixteenth of the Persian month of Azar (16 Azar), marked National Student Day in Iran.

The day commemorates the deaths of three students killed by the Shah's regime on 16 Azar in 1953. Richard Nixon, then the vice president of the United States, was visiting Tehran less than four months after a CIA-engineered coup d'etat that overthrew Prime Minister Mohammad Mossadegh in August 1953. As prime minister, Mossadegh had sought since 1951 to reduce the semiabsolute role of the Shah under the 1906 constitution. He had nationalized the oil industry whose vast reserves and refinery in Abadan in southern Iran had been under British ownership (the Anglo-Iranian Oil Company, known today as BP). The CIA-led coup in Iran at the height of the Cold War was meant to rescind Mossadegh's move and to surrender Iran, once again, to Western rule.[10]

When in 1953 Tehran University students demonstrated against Nixon's visit, the Shah's "Immortal Guard" (the core members of his Imperial Guard, modeled after the French Republican Guard) entered the university campus and brutally attacked them. The date has since been an occasion to commemorate Iranian students' struggle against dictatorship and the student movement's unremitting stand for social justice.[11] Since the establishment of the Islamic Republic, the state itself has organized official national marches on this day and the student movement has initiated unofficial demonstrations, in both of which the secular and the religious participate.

16 Azar, 2009: Citizen journalists calling in to radio stations in the United States from public phones on the streets of Tehran reported quiet protests and a heavy presence of the government's armed forces on the ground. In the scattered demonstrations around the capital, the Iranian flag appeared, but everywhere, apparently, without bearing the symbol of the Islamic Republic. Demonstrators carried coffins. They chanted the state-sponsored "Down with America!" and too the 2009 protest chant *"Allah-o-akbar!"*

Eyewitnesses reported that mobile phones were being confiscated in the streets. Live blogs registered frequent attacks as reports came in of crowds breaking into song. They noted that small fires lit to protect protestors from teargas were regularly extinguished by the security forces.[12] The main gate of Tehran University was cordoned off, and it was impossible to see what was happening on university grounds. Citizen journalists said, however, that students were being taken away in ambulances, probably as a cover for arrests that were happening on the campus.

In the midst of these demonstrations, a student at Tehran's Amir Kabir University of Technology, Majid Tavakoli, was arrested after giving "a fiery speech denouncing dictatorship."[13] Following his arrest, a photograph of Tavakoli in a full-length black chador over a blue *hijab* was published by official news agencies, announcing that he had attempted to flee security forces dressed in women's clothing.

Fars News mounted his image next to a photograph of the first president of the Islamic Republic, Abol-Hasan Bani-Sadr, taken after his deposition in 1981. Having betrayed his nation, Bani-Sadr had reportedly escaped Iran in a woman's veil and taken asylum in Paris. The past-present dialectics formulated in the juxtaposition of these two portraits would suggest that Tavakoli's situation was similar to Bani-Sadr's. Cowardly, he had attempted to escape arrest in women's attire.

Majid Tavakoli after his arrest. (*Source:* http://www.farsnews.com/newstext.php?nn=8809171089)

#IamMajid avatars. Thousands of Iranian men all over the world donned the veil, and with faces bare and unpixelated took snapshots of themselves using these forebears of the #selfie as their social media avatars on Twitter and Facebook.

Online, #iranelection cried an anguished "No!" Fully cognizant that the veiled portrait of Majid Tavakoli was an attempt at ridicule—associating Tavakoli's courage with the affects of "the weaker sex"—thousands of Iranian men all over the world donned the veil, took snapshots of themselves with their laptops, and posted these on the internet, sometimes using these forebears of the #selfie as their social media avatars on Twitter and Facebook.[14]

In captioning their photographs and posting comments to their Facebook profiles, these men in scarves claimed their solidarity with Iranian women, who they emphasized have no choice but to veil under the rule of a rigid theocracy. They voiced too their opposition to the human rights violations of the Islamic Republic and called for the immediate release of Majid Tavakoli, now imprisoned. As they joined together in global solidarity under the umbrella "Majid," their campaign came to be known as the "Men's Scarves Movement" or as #IamMajid.

#IAMMAJID

There is a truth that is often shrouded in the chronicles of history. It is that upheavals and revolutions have consistently failed to achieve their goals once the so-called opposition has come to power. This is as true of the Algerian War of Independence in the 1950s as it is the Iranian Revolution of the 1970s and the Egyptian Revolution of 2011. Historically, when women have taken to the streets in these revolts, shoulder to shoulder with their men in Algeria, in Iran, and in Egypt, it has been they, the women, who when victory was won were forgotten and once again banished to their apartments. Assia Djebar's *Fantasia: An Algerian Cavalcade* speaks about this in a haunting poetics that is as powerful today as it was when she lamented the losses of the Algerian anticolonial war. The documentary made by a group of French feminists only a month after the end of the Iranian Revolution, on Women's Day in March 1979, and the audio archives consisting of the American feminist Kate Millett's interviews during that period document Iranian women too speaking to this issue with equal amounts of frustration. Preparing for her trip to Iran to speak to the crowds of women assembled for weeklong demonstrations around Women's Day, Kate Millett records a conversation with friends in her Lower East Side apartment in Manhattan: "[Women] are flocking into the streets, you know. They're really taking part in this." "Yeah, and they're gonna get screwed like we always do. . . . How many times have we put ourselves at the barricades for male revolution- aries imagining it was going to be our freedom won right along with theirs. Remember Algeria?"

In the midst of their antiveiling demonstrations against Ayatol- lah Khomeini's new edict requiring the veil for women in civic positions, the women who joined Women's Day underscored that their participation in the Revolution implicitly stood for a demand for equality on all legal and social matters. This included the continued right to hold public office, but also the choice to veil or not.

In these demonstrations women mingled—veiled and unveiled—crying out in slogans: "We fought the Shah with and without the veil! We'll fight for our freedom with and without the veil!" and "Independence, Freedom, Real Republic" (for video, scan QR code on this page). These moments marked the dawn of freedom on the heels of a lengthy insurrection against the Shah's regime. Khomeini had already arrived in Iran. And the referendum that would establish the Islamic Republic of Iran was still in the works.

While Millett herself admitted that she had seen nothing like the scope and character of the protests she witnessed in Iran, the

 women's protests, which continued for several days after Womten's Day, were strongly criticized for "causing unnecessary fraction within the social body." In order to maintain the national character of a hard-won revolution, it was thought imperative that women "*not* voice their opposition." Not demand freedom for women. Not demand freedom from a mandatory veil. Not demand the freedom of speech. Not demand the same rights as men. Not reclaim their positions in public office. Not claim their freedom of assembly. Not seek solidarity with other women. "In other words," as Sara Mameni observes, "women were asked to swallow their losses for the sake of a collective cause that did not acknowledge their grievances. This form of political loss is what we might describe as melancholia, an incorporation without recognition."[15] The process of melancholia in Abraham and Torok's rereading of Freud, writes Ranjana Khanna, reflects an "accumulated loss."[16] It "involves not a regurgitation, but a buried shared secret: the failure of the nation to assimilate its subjects in spite of its overt policy. '*Incorporation results from those losses that for some reason cannot be*

QR Women's Day demonstrations in Tehran, Iran. (Video, 1979) http://www.sup.org/mottahedeh/III14/

acknowledged as such.' The words that cannot be uttered, the scenes that cannot be recalled, the tears that cannot be shed—everything will be swallowed along with the trauma that led to the loss. Swallowed and preserved. Inexpressible mourning erects a tomb inside the subject."[17] The unprecedented protests that gave voice to Iranian women's losses in the early days after the revolution would be quelled—indeed, in the fullest expression of melancholic incorporation, swallowed—for the sake of national unity. Ingesting their "political subjectivity at the level of the flesh, [and] creating an embodied archive of their political desires," Iranian women would carry these losses under the veil, from this generation to the next.[18]

During the Algerian War of Independence (the most memorable scenes of *The Battle of Algiers* remind us), it was the *veil* that was snatched from the bodies of women for the sake of the emergent nation. Men donned veils to hide weapons, and women in turn walked "naked" (unveiled) in the streets of Algiers to accomplish various missions "dressed" as European women in the Quartiers. The use of the veil as a technology, as both armor and weapon, is not new in the context of opposition. In Iran it dates back beyond the Bábí movement of the nineteenth century, in which Tahirih Qurrat al-'Ayn is said to have unveiled in an assembly of eighty-two men to call an end to the laws and institutions of Islam.[19]

Placed then in the proper light of this history and in the blinding glare of a bloody struggle for civil and human rights in Iran, it would be foolish to misrecognize the quiet show of strength and resilience embodied by "the men in scarves" as a gesture of "postmodern transvestism." In the face of brutal force, with faces bare, unpixelated, and unprotected for the first time since the first quiet glimmerings of hope in the early postelection days, the "Majids" posed in scarves and veils before their digital cameras. In one brave stroke these veiled men showed their resistance to an enforced gender apartheid, indeed their opposition to a state that consistently violates human rights. In this one gesture they joined their voices with other men to express their desire for an expanded sphere of civil liberties in Iran. Thirty years after the women's protests in March 1979 these "men in scarves" arrived to stand proudly next to their sisters and mothers who had been at the forefront of the movement for basic freedoms and rights for all since the early years of the last century. Cognizant, in the words of the great Persian modernist 'Abdu'l-Bahá 'Abbás "that until woman and man recognize and realize equality, social and political progress here or anywhere will not be possible. For the world of humanity consists of two parts or members: one is woman; the other is man. Until these two members are equal in strength, the oneness of humanity cannot be established, and the happiness and felicity of mankind will not be a reality."[20]

As Shirin Ebadi noted in an open letter posted on a feminist website, the brave Majids "demonstrated with their symbolic act that they are against laws that discriminate against women in the Islamic Republic." Indeed, she wrote in praise, "you have not only defended your imprisoned friend, you have defended womanhood. You men said by veiling yourselves that women are your equals. One complete, not half a human being!" "You shouted that you respect your mothers and defend the human rights of your sister," she wrote. "By veiling yourselves, you men defended the Human Rights of your sisters!" For this act of courage, she added, "I am proud to say that you are part of the movement for women's rights in Iran!"[21]

It is this solidarity in desire and spirit that has been taking shape in the private sanctuary of the home, not (at least not just) the longing to undress. As Haleh Anvari eloquently puts it:

> For 22 years, since I returned after living in Britain, I have seen women push against boundaries in every aspect of life. We have established a distance between the realities of our lives and how the state wishes us to behave. We have consistently defied official efforts to keep us inside our private spaces, by entering universities and professions in record numbers. But it is also in the sanctuary of our private spaces that we have raised young men and women who now can negotiate conservative cultural norms more smoothly than we ever did before the revolu-

tion. Many Iranian women still fight for tangible legal equalities; supported by many of our menfolk, we often pay dearly in that effort, whether we wear the chador or the manteau.[22]

Within the private spheres of kinship, this alignment between men and women has been practiced and daily perfected. This solidarity in vision and strength was felt emphatically in the #Iam-Majid campaign's global impact. The campaign eventually went live in several cities, and YouTube videos documented it.

The most moving of these digital videos is of a group of Iranian men in Paris. Young and old, mustached and clean-shaven, six men dressed in black-on-blue full-length *hijab*s appear in the frame of the minute-long You-Tube video, one by one, to the beat of the artist Mohsen Namjoo's musical reinterpretation of Hafiz's Persian poem "Zolf Bar Bad Made." They pose together in the final shot of the  video, wrapped tightly in their chadors, standing in front of the Eiffel Tower (for video, scan QR code on this page).

This act of resistance to the violation of fundamental human rights and liberties in Iran had stunning reverberations in France where French men and women too donned the veil in solidarity with the Iranian "men in scarves," and in this simple gesture, which went viral in social media, showed their opposition to *l'affaire du voile* in France.[23]

In April 2013, a group of men in the Kurdistan province of Iran launched a similar social media campaign after police arrested and subjected a Kurdish man to humiliation by forcing him to march in public dressed in traditional Kurdish women's clothing.

#SELFIE

From kitty selfies to the Syrian jihadist selfies, from the #obamaselfie at Mandela's memorial event in 2013,[24] to the selfies taken

QR "We are all Majid Tavakoli" at the Eiffel Tower in Paris. (Video, 2009) http://www.sup.org/mottahedeh/III17/

in the midst of daily life by soldiers in the Israeli Defense Force,[25] netizens live a cultural life a previous generation would have called self-centered and narcissistic. But as the impact of Soltani's profile picture on Facebook and the political force of the #IamMajid campaign imply, this is not only a misreading of the nature and function of the #selfie (and the psychoanalytic formulation of narcissism to boot); it is also a misrecognition of the selfie's aesthetic, technological, commercial, and social history.

Added to the *Oxford Dictionary Online* in August 2013, "selfie" is "catchall term for digital self-portraits abetted by the explosion of cellphone cameras and photo-editing and sharing services." Posted to Twitter in response to collective viewing events, popular television shows or sporting events for example, "the selfie is much more like your face is the caption and you're trying to explain a moment or tell a story," says Frédéric della Faille. In this digital ecology, the selfie is far more effective as relay than text ever could be, allowing others to see and experience the moment, the thought, and the space of the experience simultaneously, that is, as they too are having their own experiences. As the hashtag that is attached to it suggests, the #selfie is "much more complex than a snapshot." It feeds on "an amalgam of processed visual data, descriptive tags, and the particular social network into which it is launched."[26]

With 150 million users, that network is usually Instagram. Aggregating their images using hashtags, users can choose to share the images publicly or privately from within that network. More than fifty million images are uploaded daily with slew of descriptive hashtags that also contextualize and differentiate the images, which on Instagram are often glanced at, "rather than pored over,"[27] on a small digital screen. Here the digital images feel more like text messages or tweets. Associated with the ephemeral, the trivial, the routine, the everyday, the unconscious, the unremarkable, as the exact antithesis of what has routinely been called "history," the selfie is connected in its quotidianness to the lives of women and to private life. In its daily coarticulation with objects invested with power, it stands to challenge all contemporary notions of the state, of government, of capital, of art and urban design, of copyright, and of privacy. In this, it confronts ideas of the beautiful and the presentable as well. It is in this sense that the selfie aligns with the quotidian body of the collective, as opposed to, say, the body of the monarch (a double body which, as Foucault significantly points out, is the traditional subject of historical chronicles), and with the emergence on the global stage of "the people" as the selfie's urform.

THE URFORM

In his historical overview of the emergence of "the people" in Iranian political life, Setrag Manoukian observes that "the history of Iran is constellated with 'riots.' The Constitutional Revolution of 1905–1911 witnessed

> the emergence of "the crowd" as a political category, calling for a constitutional monarchy. The shah had ruled over "subjects" (ra'iyat), the Shi'i jurisprudents and theologians had guided "followers" (moqalled), and the learned had distinguished themselves from the "commoners" ('âm). These categories were substantially altered through the fragmented and often contradictory encounter among the Iranian arts of government, the concepts of European political modernity, and the impingement of Britain and Russia. In the wake of this process of conceptual dislocation, crowds on the streets catalyzed the formation of their counterpoint, "the people" (mardom), who were named at once the victim of tyranny, the embodiment of a national and/or religious community, and the needy to be taken care of and educated.[28]

During the early days of the Iranian election crisis, it was "the people" who occupied the streets and boulevards of the city and who attempted to distinguish themselves from the "riff raff," [29] the "soccer fans," the "thugs," and "the hooligans" of the state's rhetoric about them. They were Iranians, workers, students. They were brothers, and sisters. Together they were unafraid. They were "the people." "The relevance of the people has endured for thirty years," writes Manoukian, since the establishment of the Islamic

Republic. And "years of disciplinary exercise, the war against Iraq, and an intensive project of technological and infrastructural development continuously turned the crowds of the revolution into the people of the Islamic Republic."

Yet, and this is crucial, "During the presidential campaign of 2009, all candidates claimed to be the true representatives of the people. In televised debates, President Ahmadinejad argued that he always acted 'in service to the people,' while his opponent Mir-Hossein Mousavi argued that Ahmadinejad's cabinet was a shame for the people." "In the aftermath of the fraudulent election, political figures and religious ones too, made reference to the people and claimed allegiance to them, while condemning their enemies, despite different identifications of what 'the people' were. Ahmadinejad defined crowds as either 'foreign agents' or 'rabble,' praising security forces for reestablishing order for the people."[30]

The opposition defended "the people," its color (green), its voice (Neda). "*Rang-e ma, rang-e Ma! Neda-ye Ziba-ye ma*" (Our color, our color! Our beautiful voice/Neda). "The people" were the ones who expressed their dissatisfaction with the death of (some) Iranians and insisted that there should be no fear in their being on the streets. They were there together after all. The slogans "*Irani mimirad, zellat nemipazirand*" (Iranians rather die than tolerate humiliation) and "*Natarsid, natarsid! Ma hame ba ham hastim!*" (Don't be afraid, don't be afraid! We are all together!) were regularly chanted by the protestors as an expression of their unity and solidarity. The people worked diligently to identify the police, the security forces, the "paid agents," the *basij* or militia (often referring to them as the "plainclothes") in texts, videos, and images, which were uploaded to blogs and circulated in tweets. *They* were the enemy of the people who were occupying the boulevards, the streets, and the squares of the Revolution. Sometimes the people went further, insisting that the hired guns had non-Iranian accents, Arabic accents, that they were from Lebanon, that they couldn't be Iranians, that such savagery couldn't be of "the people." These themes were also echoed in the nationalism of the most abhorrent of the 2009 slogans "*Na

"Plainclothes" Iranian security forces taking photographs of the protestors. (*Source:* http://www .radiofarda.com/media/photogallery/1901633.html)

Gaza Na Lebnan Janam fadaye Iran" (Neither Gaza, nor Lebanon, I give my life for Iran) and the more pernicious "*Nejade ma aryast-deen, az siasat jodas*" (We are an Aryan race, religion and politics don't mix), in which the denial of racial kinship with the Arab world aimed to profile the secular, and in this equation of belonging, accentuate the ties that bind "the people" to an Aryan European filial past.

Such attempts to separate the good from the bad in the political discourse and the slogans of the period often led to missteps, for as numerous reports by citizen journalists underscored, the distinctions between the people, the riot police, and members of the Revolutionary Guard were foggy at best. Protestors were regularly rescuing wounded guards and members of the police force from the marching mass, offering them water and medical help. Early tweets by @persiankiwi suggested the defection of ranking members of the Revolutionary Guard, and police testified to protestors on several occasions of their unwillingness to attack "the people."[31]

As Manoukian argues, in 2009 "the people" appeared as "a mobile, heterogeneous milieu of potentiality" that no "socioeconomic or ideological typology seems to grasp." Defined more by its mimetic gestures and viral composition, "the people" emerged in 2009 as an amorphous collective sensorium articulated with and networked to others at a distance elsewhere. In this collusion with gestures of a frail corporality and in the contagion perpetuated online and off through their mimetic practices, one reads in "the people" a networked term. There is a persistent virality, indeed a paradigm of survival, that underscores the relevance, the significance, and finally the reflexive way in which "the people" represented, in embodied form, the collective life elsewhere that was also spreading it and pulsing through its networked appearance as meme.

#TBT

In the summer of 2009, Golbarg Bashi and I had a lengthy conversation about a set of photographs from historical Iranian protests. A talented Swedish-Iranian photographer and feminist herself, she had assembled the photoset around images of women and asked my thoughts about them.[32] The photos depicted protesting Iranian women over the decades—1951, 1978, and 2009.[33] The first was taken in Tehran on the heels of the nationalization of the Anglo-Iranian Oil Company by Prime Minister Mohammad Mossadegh. The next two were taken during the massive street protests that started in 1977 and that resulted in the revolution that established the Islamic Republic of Iran in March 1979. The last two were digital images that circulated online on social media platforms during the postelection uprising of 2009. The images stood for three iconic periods in Iranian history in which women were at the forefront of movements for change. We began discussing the photoset via email as violence was breaking out on city streets and immediately following the circulation of the digital video of Neda Agha-Soltan's death. What might these images teach us about the present?

Women protesting for the nationalization of oil under British control in Iran, July 1, 1951.
(© Dmitri Kessel/The LIFE Picture Collection/Getty Images)

Women demonstrating during Iranian Revolution, 1978. (© Christine Spengler/Sygma/Corbis)

Women protesting during the anti-Shah demonstrations, 1979. (*Source:* http://www.pbs.org/wgbh/pages/frontline/tehranbureau/2009/07/picturing-ourselves-1953-1979-and-2009.html)

Women protesting during the Iranian postelection crisis, 2009. (© AP/Ben Curtis)

Female supporters of Mir-Hossein Mousavi in front of Tehran University in Tehran, Iran, on Wednesday, June 3, 2009. (© Ramin Talaie/Corbis)

Read chronologically, the photographs clearly point to the integral role of women in social movements in Iran over time. They do so indexically, one could say, in that something fundamental to the moment of the event touches the film itself, recording the light that is reflected on the women's bodies as they march beneath banners of protest or raise their fists in opposition. The photographs, as fossilized light, establish a material and archeological fact, namely that the active presence of protesting women in the viral pixelated images from the streets in 2009 is not something new.

The dialectical relationship between movements and the technologies that mediate them is both immediate and striking from the set as well. In studying the photograph taken during the 1951 demonstrations and the ones representing the people's revolution against the ruling monarchy in 1978 and 1979, it is obvious that the camera stands separate and distant from the protestors. One could say, in this sense, that the camera is familiar with the patterns of classical political organization and the photo ops that such demonstrations would provide. The camera stands at a distance, flattening its separation from the mass, and only brings the events closer by means of its choice of lens and angle. It then retreats to the safety of diplomatic immunity in order to communicate its messages to recipients elsewhere. The camera is in a space that is separate, both ideologically and ethnographically. In that sense the camera in 1951 documents a moment of confrontation with a power elsewhere. It speaks, indeed, of a Third Worldism, a moment that is, for now, of the past.

The 1951 photograph speaks too of the people's clear understanding of a specific embodied and material form of ideological protest. Bodies move under banners, in patterns of organized demonstrations one often associates with labor protests. One could argue that the camera of the 1951 photograph is critically bound to the forms and functions of the protests it captures, and to the residual patterns linked to forms of power that no longer hold. The 1951 photograph speaks of a firm anti-imperialism, an embodied collectivism, an indigenous nationalism, and of a time when the oppressive force of power remained outside, impacting everyday life but from afar. It is interesting to note, for example, that in the absence of a large archive of digital images posted by the participants in the antiveiling street protests in France in 2010, news media documented the protests like the camera of the 1951 photograph would.[34] In these 2010 news reports, banners speak overhead on behalf of the disciplined mass of bodies moving in unison beneath them. What is significantly different in the 2010 photographs from France, however, is the camera's tight framing around the mass, a framing that also seems to entrap the assembled protestors under these banners. The closed shot of a teaming crowd, claustrophobic at best, suggests a biased attempt in the camera work itself to cast *l'affaire du voile* in the trappings of a former era. As if to brush the whole affair off as something archaic or, rather, passé.

A manicured hand about to throw a stone during clashes with police in Tehran on Saturday, June 13, 2009. (© Ahmed Jadallah/Reuters/Corbis)

For if we observe the framing and distance of the 1951 photograph, a journalistic professionalism, objectivity, and remove speak from within it. A long shot and a wide-angle lens capture the avenue filled with protesting bodies. In 2009, the professionalism of this lens was categorically reframed as netizens circulated viral content on social media and as journalists assumed a different role, that of the expert talking head on news shows, reflecting in sound bites on the state of politics and the structures of power. The camera that captured the people's uprising in Iran in 2009, obviously digital and handheld, was awkwardly absent in the 2010 news photographs in France, as if it didn't yet know how to walk alongside the protestors or, more pointedly, refused to do so. In Iran, by contrast, it moved with the crowd:

A sudden close-up of cement blocks appears in someone's hand. The camera moves to people walking in sparse groups or by themselves. At a street corner a young woman offers more pieces of cement blocks to those passing by, including the holder of the video camera, who stops for a second or two before moving again, framing some who walk in the opposite direction, a burning trash can, the trees that line the street. Slogans are interrupted by commentaries, then after moments of silence and movement, shots are heard as the camera nears an intersection and frames the street sign. A voice reads the name of the street out loud as if announcing it to an audience and adds, "They are shooting real bullets," and everything starts to move faster; a group of people passes by carrying someone wounded, while everyone cries and runs, and then the camera stops again to zoom in on a pool of blood. The video captures the mixture of casualness, confusion, and purposefulness in a crowd whose participants move from laughter to crying and outrage, only to become again passersby and spectators.[35]

The pixelated viral images of the 2009 camera are thoroughly implicated by "the people." Their textures meme the camera's closeness to the events, communicating an immediacy and affinity with others, who, inhabiting a space elsewhere, experience the events simultaneously.[36] This composition, more properly a configuration perhaps, speaks volumes of the camera's instant and subjective collusion with the premises of the gestures it captures, the affinities it assumes, and the immediacy and virality of its embodied response to the events it witnesses.

On the streets and boulevards of 2009, the people are at once "commanders, defenders, martyrs, and journalists." They are characterized by a spatiotemporal awareness of simultaneity and a persistent mimetics. This sensory continuity and temporal immediacy of experience online and offline is evident to anyone on social media today. But that sensation of continuity, between the body and digital technology, only first became palpable, historically speaking, in the midst of the social protests in Iran in 2009. It was not until the uprisings in the Arab world in the spring of 2011 that the intimation of the experience many had had during #iranelection became evident globally. Imagine this now rather common scenario: A protestor running away from the security forces falls. She hurts her leg and bleeds. Her stained skin pierces through her jeans, but her mobile phone is broken too. The throbbing discomfort of the fall slows her pace and her connection to the protesting crowd. But the fall simultaneously disrupts her feed, and her continuous access to a network of friends and supporters who stand in solidarity with her online from a distance elsewhere. A mimesis is embedded in this immediacy of experience that was initially sensed collectively in the 2009 crisis in Iran as the first populist revolt to enlist and engage social media on a global scale. That historical moment in the life of the sensing body of the collective shaped the landscape of social media and the assumptions that we now bring to our experience as we connect online today. Writes Manoukian:

> In this new social figure, protesting and reporting, two positions usually considered distinct, become indistinguishable. Protesting was a sign of presence in a crowd. Reporting was in varying degrees removed from crowds in the figure of either a "reporter" who was not part of them or a "witness" narrating events after the fact. Once, mediation followed action and translated it into language. Now the two dimensions are simultaneous. The "citizen-journalist" is at once acting and reporting on his or her own actions and those of others. This inextricable combination of action and mediation establishes new spatiotemporal coordinates. Protests and their media become intertwining aspects of the same event.[37]

In this elaborate weave, part flesh part data, they point "toward new configurations of the relationship between politics and experience."[38]

#HAIRDONE

Significant in the comparison of the photographs of Iranian women is the sartorial choices of the protestors. The fashions in particular speak volumes. In the photograph from 1951, some men wear European hats. Women in full-length black chadors walk shoulder to shoulder with women wearing dresses that are influenced by the Western fashions of the time. Women's hair is Rita Hayworth-esque.[39] And while men and women of different backgrounds and ideological persuasions participated in the uprising against the Pahlavi monarchy and, too, revolted against his forced Westernization of Iran, the fashion on the streets is unironically reflexive of 1970s Western sartoriality. This is especially evident in the photographs from the winter of 1978–79 (see page 88).

We are certain to notice a uniformity in the coiffure and dress of the 1950s photograph, and too of the 1970s photographs, but given the government-enforced veiling of women, the uniformity in dress in the 2009 photographs is bound to feel very different. Rather than the fashion-catalogue sameness of the outfits in the

Women at a rally in downtown Tehran, Iran, Monday, June 8, 2009, dressed in green, the color of the Mousavi campaign. (© AP Photos/Vahid Salemi)

earlier photographs, in the 2009 photographs the young women, especially, show a desire to alter a given uniform. Donned with green ribbons, the state-enforced Islamic uniform playfully reveals a strand of hair, a corporality, a provocation.

Arriving at Mehrabad airport in Tehran following the revolutionary insurrection of the Iranian people, Millett noted how Iranian women defied everything:

I suddenly remember[ed] them myself, how these two amazing females in the brassiest outfits had taken the whole somber airport by storm. So strumpet. Their costume actually a costume, out-harloting every cliché and arriving at a work of art. Highest heels, the flimsiest skirts, hair dyed and flying in the wind as they raced in and shouted the names of their arrivals. Nothing in the world intimidated them, not the chador, not the guns. "Real outlaws, I loved them." "You see them somewhere else and you'd think—my, how ridiculous." "Like Punkers," Sophie[40] [Millett's companion] muse[d]. "Like punk rock and CBGB they looked." "The lipstick, the tight clothes. Nail polish. They become gestures of defiance, not just imperialist Western decadence and so forth. For them, in that room, that uptight atmosphere, the guns and the chador—they're a way to say, 'Fuck you.' Man, when they went through that airport, they defied. Everything. You and I are just in the wrong place with the wrong clothes on. They actually got dressed up to do that number." "Like faggots wearing a dress to a parade." "It's deliberate, subversion. Revolutionary. And that wonderful one welcoming her lover, she jumped right up on his waist, with her legs around his waist, he twirled around and around and they kissed and kissed. . . . These two gorgeous apparitions, this Marseilles tart and her sailor man, were like the circus, like fun, like it could be fun to be alive and untied and celebrate a revolution and dance in the street if that fool with his machine gun would move away from the door.

The Islamic Republic gained its distinction and identity by addressing itself precisely to this: to the body and the senses. As the March 1979 protests that were documented in Millett's archives testify, Khomeini's new regime would conceive a new psychical structure for the new nation and do so by aiming strict regulations on the bodies of women.[41] These bodies became the symbols and symptoms of the Shi'ih state. The Social Morality Plan (*tarh-e amniyat ejtema'i*) established by Ahmadinejad in 2006 was "an attempt to re-impose the rigid codes of dress and comportment that prevailed in the earliest days of the revolution."[42] There followed every summer warnings about women's states of exposure and repeated threats of arrest for women showing up in public "suntanned . . . like walking mannequins."[43]

> Bracelets, necklaces, extraordinary haircuts, western graphic tees, and long hair that once landed men in the pound have largely been thrown out the window because today, the morality police has evolved to almost exclusively target women. For them, pushing boundaries once meant donning colorful outfits and light makeup in the early years after the 1979 revolution. Then came boots—some recall former president Akbar Hashemi Rafsanjani's chador-clad daughter making headlines with her high-tops in the mid-90s. During the Khatami era in the late 90s and early 2000s, Iranian women speak of Capri pants, shorter manteaus, and more exposed hair. But hardliners tried to roll back as much of that as possible when conservative Ahmadinejad took office . . . women were fined for each individual painted fingernail. But still, even as the morality police units grew in number, manteaus continued to grow progressively shorter and tighter, sleeves shrank, and a new technique emerged to hang the headscarf on a small, pointy bun on the back of women's heads. These days, hardliners are riled by exposed ears, "leggings," and robe-like "open" manteaus.[44]

In the relentless corporality of the protests of 2009, one hears the rustling leaves of an archive of melancholy, an archive of catastrophic political losses, "swallowed" and carried in the bodies of women from the dawn of the new revolutionary state.

#INSTALOVE

The manicured nails, the threaded eyebrows, the strand of hair that shows on the veiled forehead are all markers of bodily revolt in public space. Indeed, they are acts of corporal and sexualized defiance that have been incorporated, policed by the state, then reinvented and re-embodied over and over again since 1981 when the system of modesty regulating heterosexual relations and the veiling of women finally became mandatory in the Islamic Republic.[45] The repetition of this logic of action and reaction, intrinsic to the act of both citation and melancholia, as Khanna argues, "installs a moment of stasis . . . [W]hen the inorganic past or that which is lost, is brought into the present, this drive toward stasis . . . holds within it an attempt to assimilate its meaning into another context."[46] In the age of viral reality, the melancholic failure to assimilate a history of political loss is memed elsewhere. It circulates as a residue of state policies in "the longing" bodies of women and men:

> It's afternoon at Park-e Laleh, a popular destination for students who attend one of central Tehran's sprawling universities. Seated on a bench under tall trees, Mandana, 22 and Daniel, 34, pose for selfies taken with Mandana's iPhone. While many of these images will end up on Mandana's Facebook and Instagram pages, the couple keeps the more intimate shots to themselves. Even in the leafy nooks of the park, there are rules to observe, and the unmarried pair is never completely alone. Taking selfies allows them to create virtual moments of privacy. "We feel like just the two of us present."[47]

In the 2009 election aftermath, wives of key reformist figures who were taken as political prisoners wrote open letters to their husbands. These were posted online and were available for public reflection. As Ziba Mir-Hosseini notes, "What makes these often very affecting love letters especially significant is that many of the writers are women from religious backgrounds who now have no qualms about speaking of their physical longing for their men."[48] Questioning the system that has unjustly imprisoned their men, they mournfully give expression to a corporal longing and sexual desires that through the early political loss of voice after the Iranian Revolution were ingested into their bodies as melancholia. Clearly, Mir-Hosseini reflects, the policies of the Islamic Republic have generated a paradox. "Having politicized the sexuality and honor of all Iranian women," by enforcing veiling on all, a matter previously assigned to the family and local community, "the regime now finds its own adherents taking the policies' spirit to an uncomfortable extreme."[49] But there really is no surprise in this. For as Joan Copjec remarks, what shame defines as an affect is a woman's relation to her own culture. "To the extent that the *hejab* system encourages subjects to experience their interiority, their privacy, as being intact even while they are in a public place, as many Muslims attest, then it certainly safeguards shame. . . . To the extent, however, that the *hejab* system forbids or impedes any of its citizens access to publicity, it strips them of the possibility of experiencing shame. Under these conditions no architectural barrier, no veil, or chador will suffice to protect a citizen's modesty. Rather than protecting women from exposure, the limitation of their access to public forums can only turn them inside out, externalize them completely."[50]

The dialectics of interiority evident in the examples of Iranian women's digital presence in 2009 are expressive of a corporality that is nowhere to be found in that sense of "properness" that is alive in the "pretty" floral dresses and the "nice sunglasses" of the women who quietly marched under banners in the 1951 photograph. The distance from that moment is evident in the posture of a young woman about to throw a stone (see photo on opposite page), where we are witness to an undeniable element of a corporality, a bodily confrontation, "a coming face-to-face" with security forces in public space. Here, by virtue of the positioning of the camera alongside the protestor's body, that is, in the alignment of our look with the camera's look, our own corporality as viewers is implicated and networked. This kind of alignment is largely

A woman about to throw a stone during a street protest in Tehran on June 20, 2009, defying an ultimatum from the Supreme Leader Ayatollah Ali Khamenei for an end to protests. (© AFP/Getty Images)

absent in the photographs of earlier periods. Indeed one could say that a certain corporality is deemphasized by the "objective" distance of the 1950s and 1970s camera and by the sartorial choices, which either situate themselves within the flows of commercial capital and global fashion or squarely take a stand against the same by virtue of the chador. While we must be vigilant in remembering the presence of young women in militant guerrilla movements such as Cherikha-ye Fada'i Khalaq or Mujahedyn-e Khalq in the 1970s and 1980s, what we witness in the photographs of the 2009 protests is the ordinariness of a gesture which is stripped of all but frustration: a young woman readied to "throw a stone with manicured hand." Stalwart, this image speaks allegorically of an archived melancholy that spans decades of political loss on the public front for Iranian women in protest.

#SOLIDARITY

In his remarks about the nude photograph of Golshifteh Farahani, the first Iranian star to appear in a Hollywood film, Hamid

Dabashi rightly observes that neither she nor the Egyptian blogger Aliaa Magda Elmahdy, who posed nude on her blog against the effects of societal violence, racism, sexism, harassment, and hypocrisy, were the first Muslim women to pose naked in recent memory and to publicize it:

> Long before them, another young Iranian woman, Minou Arjomand, joined an HIV/AIDS advocacy group ACT UP for a top-to-toe naked demonstration outside Madison Square Garden in New York City, where the Republican National Convention was taking place in August 2004, protesting against President Bush's AIDS policies. She and her friends later posed for a group portrait that was published in the New Yorker magazine.[51]

Dabashi observes that the ACT UP photograph was taken before social media networks such as Twitter and Facebook "turned the world inside out." That may be true. It does indeed account for the lack of wide-scale awareness of this courageous and historic act of embodied political defiance, in which, as Dabashi writes, "Minou Arjomand joined that group portrait in protest at President Bush's HIV/AIDS policies without any pomp or ceremony, and without the slightest publicity drawn to that photo beyond the limited HIV/AIDS epidemic activist circles." But it would be equally true to say that in the corporal emphasis that this analog photograph of the collective brings to a biological virus, it foreshadows, as urform, that immediacy of experience and affinity of sensorial transmission that my discussion of the networked term, "the people," has underscored. There is, in other words, more to the correlation of corporality, virality, and social media than Dabashi's remarks regarding the ACT UP photograph acknowledge. As a media object, the group photograph anticipates the collectivity, the corporality, and the virality of the online ecology that is on its immediate horizon.

Here, the figure of the young woman readied to "throw a stone with manicured hand" (photo on page 99) stands as the allegorical form anticipated by the ACT UP photograph. It is allegorical in that it shuttles at once between an image of the lone woman corporally present in the midst of the crowd, and a concept: a collective elsewhere sensorially connected and networked by her image. Part flesh, part data, the figure of the young woman readied to "throw a stone with manicured hand" articulates, as allegory, a politics that hinges on the amorphous web of social media.

Clearly, we see in the 2009 photoset women (and men)—walking in protest, holding banners and placards—not unlike their historical compatriots in Iran seen in the 1950s and 1970s photographs. But the demand for individualized representation that is inscribed in textual form as "Where is my Vote?" for example, is witnessed also repeatedly as a document of a corporality that circulates, like a virus. It circulates therefore not necessarily within the domain of global capital (as with the photographs from 1951, 1978, and 1979), but within, and therefore incessantly against, a

"Where is my Vote?" A protestor with a slogan of the 2009 Iranian election crisis during a street protest on Tuesday, June 16, 2009. (© Getty Images/Stringer)

systematic and individuated regulation of the body. The camera that documents—usually digital and embedded in a handheld device—a camera that moves along with the protestors, understands the logic of these meming bodies in collective revolt. In chanting, tweeting, geo-tagging, and linking, in marching, recording, status-updating, and uploading, the documentation of these protesting bodies, in their liveness and virality, cite and meme a demand for the visibility of a collectivity denied by the ascendency of neoliberalism in the global sphere.

For as the authors of *The New Way of the World: On Neoliberal Society*, Pierre Dardot and Christian Laval, show, "Neo-liberalism is not merely destructive of rules, institutions and rights. It is also productive of certain kinds of social relations, certain ways of living, certain subjectivities." What is at stake in neoliberalism "is nothing more, nor less, than the form of our existence—the way in which we are led to conduct ourselves, to relate to others and to ourselves. . . . This norm enjoins everyone to live in a world of generalized competition; it calls upon wage-earning classes and populations to engage in economic struggle against one another; it aligns social relations with the model of the market; it promotes the justification of ever greater inequalities; it even transforms the individual, now called on to conceive and conduct him- or herself as an enterprise."[52]

Gone, in this environment, is the ability to recognize the appearance and significance of collective formations and extended solidarities. This precise elision accelerated the rise of the hashtag #CNNfail with the hashtag #iranelection on Twitter in the first few days of the mass uprising in Iran. CNN may have noted the Iranian crisis. But its failure was to eschew any real emphasis on the networked collective that emerged in the figure of "the people" in response. Here was an international and collective act of dissent against the injustices of the state, and CNN was focusing its energies and professional resources on corporate bids for bankruptcy in the United States.

If hierarchical power, as Jacques Rancière notes, "asserts that the space for circulating is nothing but the space of circulation," then "[p]olitics, by contrast, consists in transforming this space of 'moving-along,' of circulation, into a space for the appearance of a subject: the people, the workers, the citizens."[53] This subject appears. She appears in the elisions and gaps. She appears in the networked object, the #selfie. In fact she appears alongside her friends and followers, sensorially connected to viral images of embodied protest in online platforms everywhere. The dismissal of the collective dignity of this, the people, is the precise issue the #Occupy mobilization addressed in the heart of neoliberalism, by occupying public space. Connected to the corporality of a protesting collective on the ground and intimately linked to its senses by the immediacy of its mimetic reproduction of sights and sounds, social media has emerged as the site of embodied assembly on a global scale. To stand alongside those protesting by the "only means left to them— the site of their bodies, blowing it up in Palestine, Iraq or Afghanistan, burning it to ashes in Tunisia or Morocco, exposing [the body's] fragile innocence in Egypt or else in exile in Europe or the United States," as if each were a melancholic archive of loss made flesh.[54]

While social media admittedly provides the possibility for a singular voice to speak of its personal revolt (as witnessed in the cases of the Norwegian bomber, Anders Breivik, and the twenty-two-year-old gunman, Elliot Rodger, in Santa Barbara, California), it simultaneously occasions the site of coordination, cocreation, and convergence that is capable of convening an emergent "paradoxical world that puts together two separate worlds." This world is an indestructible, ever amorphous networked association, which bridges a partition that was opened up by the atomization of the worker and the disintegration of all collective structures in favor of a neoliberal utopia in which all solidarities and collaborative standards were torn down—ripped and dashed, in fact, in total disregard for the needs of the body, the senses of the worker, and the voices of the people. Social media extends the reach of the sensorially mediated subject that appears virally, now beyond the boundaries of the state and the multilateral practices that dictate its dealings with the people, to impact and involve others, mimetically, in the space of politics. These others join, collaborate, and converge both locally and remotely in nonhierarchical organizations "unconsciously modeled" on the loose "networks of the web," because they are continuously practiced and mined from within them.[55] Amorphous, flexible, and remotely networked, these creative, collective, and disorderly formations of solidarity unravel both the classical *and* the neoliberal organizations of power and privilege, illustrated most obviously by the wide-scale impact of the so-called Arab Spring in 2011, which urged Noam Chomsky to observe that "the fate of democracy is at stake in Madison, Wis., no less than it is in Tahrir Square."[56]

The global collective that was sensorially tied to the hashtag #iranelection, while unwavering in its support of the protestors in Iran and mimetically geo-tagged alongside them, stands more profoundly as an incorporated archive of global political violations. Its appearance on the world stage is symptomatic of a melancholic failure to reclaim as our own the most fundamental loss, a loss that if recognized would effectively transform all of us. The loss, to name it, is that of true kinship—of an encompassing human solidarity.

ACKNOWLEDGMENTS

Back when that broad Cheshire cat smile to the screen was still a rare sight, when there were few smartphones on the market and the "CrackBerry" was the big obsession of the business world, I was visiting my friend Michael Dila in Toronto. Over dinner, I caught him fidgeting with his phone ... and then, there it was: He gave it a big smile. When I asked him what he was looking at, he said, "Twitter." I looked at him, quite puzzled. "Aha." I had no idea what he was talking about. It was 2007, within the year that Twitter was established, and he was following the artist Laurie Anderson. We knew what "friending" was from Facebook in those early years of social media, but the notion of "following" was quite foreign. "What do you mean you're following Laurie Anderson?" I asked. "Following her where? And, exactly, why? You're here with me. Are we going somewhere?"

It wasn't until some months later, when Michael introduced me to a stunningly vivacious netizen, a generation younger than us, that the possibilities dawned on me. When Rahaf Harfoush talked to me about her work on Obama's digital campaign for presidency and all the possibilities she was envisioning for government and corporations, I remember feeling like I was actually undergoing a chemical change. That semester I joined forces on Duke's campus with Cathy Davidson and started thinking how I would put social media at the center of my teaching and learning. My film students would tweet from the classroom that year. They would blog their papers and put on a biannual film festival on Twitter (@twitfilm), the first ever Twitter film festival. On Twitter, we opened the doors of the classroom together and the students shared what they were learning with peers who weren't privileged to join them in that physical space, but would join them online, from all around the world. It seemed outrageous somehow that what we were doing was in the US newspapers and being debated on academic panels all the time. I remember insisting that we hire a "mommy blogger" to grade the course, too: Shilyh Warren, then a graduate student in the Program in Literature, had just given birth, and she knew exactly how to relate to the students online. They loved the interaction with her so much that some of them went on to enroll in her course the following semester and attend her classroom in "real life" this time. I was privileged to be part of some of the greatest transformations in the ecology of online life at the dawn of Twitter and Facebook, before Instagram and Snapchat roamed the earth, and to be in constant conscious conversation with students, colleagues, and interested peers who were as deeply engaged with what was happening as I was. The conversations I had with Michael and Rahaf, Cathy and Lina Srivastava, and no less my colleagues Kate Hayles and Laurent Dubois, were hugely influential in these moments. My brother Kasra and my mother, Faezeh Seddigh, were also early adopters. Watching them and talking with them about how they were using digital and social media also taught me to dream about possibilities that private individuals, groups, activists, governments, and corporations later adopted as part of their everyday practice. I imagine, as I continue to engage in conversations around these issues with the visionary Olivier Zitoun, that he dreams like this all the time. He opens new worlds to me.

Given the context of my engagements with social media at the time, it was quite natural for me to turn to Twitter in June 2009, the moment that fraud came up as a possibility on the day of the Iranian presidential election. Twitter was brimming with news already on June 12, and I immediately started documenting what was going on around the hashtag #iranelection. Twitter was a very small community of visionaries, innovators, bloggers, artists, educators, and other curious peeps. There were so many people I actively followed on the hashtag #iranelection, but it was precisely because they also tweeted otherwise, because they tweeted their interests, their everyday passions, their commitments, that they became part of my circle and their circles became mine, too. This network of trust and valuation set the conditions for our transmission of the minute-to-minute eyewitness updates from Iran, a transmission that blew up our feed and transformed our engagement with the platform completely: @c_defamiliaris @change_for_iran @cshirky @dariushimes @elenabrower @elizrael @findingbibi @jakejacob @jshahryar @kawrage @kwissoker @lisssnup @ltowfigh @marxculture @mbhulo @mideastyouth @nabilharfoush @naseemfaqihi @raminhossaini @rtorres @sabzbrach @sarasaljoughi @silviabauer @sladner @south south @submedina @toddicus @vattandoost inspired me during #iranelection even though they didn't always, or maybe never, tweeted the hashtag. Supported by a Faculty Research grant funded by the Arts & Sciences Council at Duke University, much of what I documented from our tweets and blogs during #iranelection in 2009–2010 is now stored in two formats online: https://negarmottahedeh.squarespace.com/ and https://storify.com/negaratduke/iranelection.

As I write tonight, I hear protestors chanting slogans outside my building in Manhattan. Within seconds of stretching my head out of the window to see them go by, I click to a video of the arrest of #NYC2Baltimore protestors streaming to my phone from a block away on Twitter's newly purchased Periscope app. We learned a great deal from each other in those early years before Twitter gained a corporate and celebrity presence. Tweeps who experienced the transformation that Twitter's young text-based platform underwent during #iranelection still talk about 2009 and of the sense of solidarity that the hashtag #iranelection created in the midst of crisis. It was that moment of hashtag solidarity, six years ago, that made the immediacy of this one and the #BaltimoreUprising, and the one for #WalterScott two weeks ago, and 2014's #EricGarner #ICant Breathe #BlackLivesMatter #HandsUpDontShoot #IfTheyGunned MeDown, and the hundreds of others in the intervening years possible. Recognizing that *we* are the black boxes, truly the only ones bearing witness to the violence of the state, citizens in Spain staged the first hologram protests against the government's new gag law—#10AHologramasLibres. In the face of brutal and unremitting police violence against black bodies in North America, *Ill Doctrine*'s Jay Smooth made the brilliant suggestion in his Walter Scott YouTube post that what we need, in fact, is *Copify*, a platform like the music streaming platform *Spotify*, that "lets us press a single button for an unlimited hi-fi recording of police misconduct." A *Copify* app that also automatically live-streams and uploads to a Cloud storage, so that, as he puts it, "they can't just snatch our phone and delete it." And frankly, he's right! "As it stands right now, when our system of policing crashes and burns, our only slim chance of justice is if we are the black box." Our only chance is that we see and hear for each other; that we stand in solidarity with each other.

In the process of thinking about social media's role in the 2009 crisis, I've had the opportunity to talk to Karim Wissa about the coincidence of #CNNfail and #iranelection, which opens the book, and to Srinivas Aravamudan, Courtney Baker, miriam cooke, Lindsey Green-Simms, Frances Hasso, Julie Poucher Harbin, Kelly Jarrett, Robert Shandley, and Ben Trott, about hashtag solidarity as a response to the workings of contemporary capital globally, and about the role of women at the forefront of major upheavals in Iran.

The serendipitous opportunity to connect and engage with Lea Muldtofte Olsen's work around the idea of a collective sensorium online arose from a single post on Facebook last summer. Lea and I haven't stopped talking since, regardless of the physical obstacles that have arrived in the form of chilling winters, missed flights, and glitchy Google hangout connections between the United States and Scandinavia, which is where we both call home. In the meantime, my friends Oz Abramovitz, Jaq Belcher, Susan James, Kyle Lohr, Windy McCracken, Amy Sexton, Rena Sherman and the Booj Meister, Khakestar, have made New York lovely. . . .

In similarly uprooted states, over distances, and in long text message exchanges, Facebook comments, and emails, but also face-to-face and in-person in Durham, NC, with Navid Naderi I have discussed the elision from the scene of #iranelection, the objects and subjects from Kurdistan that could not be memed even as they stood in solidarity with the "Sea of Green." The state violence against the Kurds is never registered as the violence of the state against its own on any #iranelection platform, as Navid has repeatedly pointed out to me, in part because of the Kurdish resistance to any assimilation towards nationalist ends. This is true of the Bahá'ís in Iran as well. The limits of the nation-state continue to dictate the limits of solidarity. And I'm grateful to Navid for showing me how the global ecology of online life is being mapped onto a colonial, racist, and corporate cartography that still embodies the prejudices of the nation-state. His prints are all over this text. And for this, and for his generous friendship, I am grateful.

I have also spent many, many hours daily since 2009 talking about social media, government, and activism in other waters, with Rebecca Stein. Her work on social media inspires me still, and it is in part because of the importance that she granted my investments in social media's historical transformations by social movements that I wrote this book. My friend Ranjana Khanna's long-standing interests in the intersection of psychoanalysis, revolution, feminism, and the visual arts in North Africa and the Middle East have also been mine. Ranji's and Rebecca's warmth and their writing have been constants in the process of my thinking through #iranelection, and so it is to my two closest friends and my most brilliant colleagues that I dedicate this book.

Returning home one winter night from a dinner with Rahaf, I tweeted that I was sure that my life had accidentally taken a miraculous turn. Placing both of her phones face down next to her elbow at dinner, Rahaf spoke to me with an eloquence that came to shape the pursuit, in my work as a cultural theorist and educator, of the possibilities opened up by digital media and Web 2.0. It was inevitable, as it always is when I am near Rahaf . . . That moment of magic changed everything.

@negaratduke
New York, New York
April 30, 2015

NOTES

1. Hiedeh Farmani, "Iranians Queue from Dawn to Have Their Say in Key Poll." *Petroleumworld.* June 12, 2009. Accessed December 2, 2014. http://www.petroleumworld.com/storyt09061202.htm.

2. "Iran's Revolutionary Guards Warn against 'Velvet Revolution.'" *Democracy Digest.* June 11, 2009. Accessed December 2, 2014. http://bit.ly/1b503Up.

3. Mir-Hossein Mousavi was the Prime Minster of the Islamic Republic of Iran, from 1981 to 1989.

4. On the ground, the first days of the protests happened more or less in an anticipatory silence. See "Tehran in a Meaningful Silence." *Tehran Avenue.* June 17, 2009. Accessed December 2, 2014. http://tehranavenue.com/tooons.php?tooonsid=36. "Iran Elections: Mousavi Supporters Protest." *The Telegraph,* June 17, 2009. Accessed April 26, 2015. http://bit.ly/1KlMDAf; "2009 Iranian Revolution—Silent Protest on June 17." YouTube. June 17, 2009. Accessed April 27, 2015. https://youtu.be/99lAhR6ZLuE.

5. By June 22, hospital sources confirmed that thousands had been injured and forty-seven killed by government forces in Tehran alone.

6. Twitter was three years into its launch (2006). Few remember this, but in 2009 Twitter was still a very basic text-based, 140 characters per tweet, medium. The hyperlinked hashtag in tweets became part of the platform later in the summer of 2009. TwitPic, yfrog, and Flickr were Twitter's primary photosharing sites before image-attachments became native to Twitter's microblogging platform.

7. "Translation of Iran Slogans and Signs-2." *CNN iReport*. June 24, 2009. Accessed December 2, 2014. http://cnn.it/1zbrHem.

8. "[Today the Word 'Iran' Is Synonymous with Righteousness and Resistance against Oppression]." *CNN iReport*. July 21, 2009. Accessed December 2, 2014. http://cnn.it/1JJlmXf. See also Kathy Riordan, "How Twitter and #Iranelection Changed Each Other." *Open Salon*. June 8, 2010. Accessed December 2, 2014. http://bit.ly/1zuyzDA.

9. Roger Cohen, "A Journalist's 'Actual Responsibility.'" *New York Times*. July 6, 2009. Accessed December 2, 2014. http://nyti.ms/1KypGoz.

10. The creative efforts that came in response to the viral video of Neda's death varied from the adaptation of the Italian antifascist song "Bella Ciao" ("Bella Ciao, Iran." YouTube. July 28, 2009. Accessed April 26, 2015. https://youtu.be/SNocyz1NRjA.

. . . to Siavash's dedication, "Neda," with accompanying scrapbook images from Neda's life. ("Siavash Official video: NEDA." YouTube. June 27, 2009. Accessed April 25, 2015. http://bit.ly/1buTqLR.

. . . and "I Can't Breathe (Neda) Rerecords" by Bruz (ft. Tiatsh & Jaz)." YouTube. Accessed April 27, 2015. http://youtu.be/Ya9mD1XP3vU.

. . . and the Abjeez and Congo Man Crew's Biyaa ("Biyaa by Abjeez & Congo Man Crew." YouTube. June 20, 2009. Accessed December 2, 2014. http://youtu.be/pdyXklHL6PE.

. . . and to Safoura Ahmadi's "Silent Volcano," which associates the story of the death of Iranian youth with the mass explosion of a volcano, a volcano that is the people onto the streets and boulevards in protest ("Silent Volcano - Iran Uprising." You-Tube. September 16, 2009. Accessed December 2, 2014. http://youtu.be/nwqdwI2ozsM).

The latter, incidentally, is a cover of Carlos Puebla's "Hasta Siempre." These are only a handful of examples from a plethora of creative works made in a multiplicity of languages to honor the #iranelection protestors in response to Neda's death.

11. "Let the Earth Bear Witness (Farsi Subtitles)." YouTube. July 2, 2009. Accessed December 2, 2014. http://youtu.be/V4Qwlk2cbq4.

12. "Michael Jackson's Death Causes Enormous Spike in AT&T Traffic." *Thaindian News*. Accessed April 26, 2015. http://bit.ly/1DOuqWv.

13. "Iran Election Video With Michael Jackson." YouTube. June 24, 2009. Accessed April 26, 2015. http://bit.ly/1PIN8Hl; "Beat It You Fanatics! Just Beat It!!!" YouTube. July 7, 2009. Accessed April 27, 2015. http://bit.ly/1PMTWnB; "Iran & Michael Jackson (Man In The Mirror)". YouTube. June 26, 2009. Accessed April 27, 2015. http://bit.ly/1FrS14T; "Michael Jackson, Basij Brutality and #iranelection" Wet Tub. July 14, 2009. Accessed April 27, 2015. http://bit.ly/1bwF8tX; "Protests in Iran-They Don't Care About Us (Michael Jackson)." http://bit.ly/1OYWyfR. "Twitter Reveals Most Discussed Topics of 2009." *Mashable*. December 15, 2009. Accessed December 2, 2014. http://on.mash.to/1zP6kj7.

I. HASHTAG

1. Citizen journalism is often associated with IndyMedia in the late 1990s and, of course, alternative press institutions of the twentieth century, but moving beyond that, my argument here attempts to emphasize the global engagement of the masses of people with the minute-to-minute reporting of unfolding events.

Twitter and other social media platforms are certainly not the birthplace of citizen journalism, but they mark new configurations of independent journalism on an international scale.

2. Kenneth Kambara, "#CNN Fail." ThickCulture RSS. June 14, 2009. Accessed April 26, 2015. http://bit.ly/1z3EhvP. Austin Heap, "Tweeting the Revolution." *Salon*. June 16, 2009. Accessed April 26, 2015. http://bit.ly/1JJmcU1; Brian Stelter, "Real-Time Criticism of CNN's Iran Coverage." *New York Times*. June 14, 2009. Accessed April 26, 2015. http://nyti.ms/w1ZyXh.

3. Dolores M. Bernal. "Twitter Users Shame CNN for Not Covering Iran Elections, Riots." *News Junkie Post*. June 13, 2009. Accessed December 1, 2014. http://bit.ly/1F8ZUos.

4. Peter Horrocks, "Stop the Blocking Now." *BBC News*. June 14, 2009. Accessed April 26, 2015. http://bbc.in/1DqWWNs. And, "Iran Election Sparks Clashes." *BBC News*. June 13, 2009. Accessed April 26, 2015. http://bbc.in/1zbTNWB.

5. "Iranian Authorities Crack Down on Media." Committee to Protect Journalists. June 15, 2009. Accessed December 1, 2014. http://cpj.org/x/2c73.

6. Brian Stelter, "Real-Time Criticism of CNN's Iran Coverage."

7. "Iran Opposition Keeps Up Pressure." *BBC News*. June 16, 2009. Accessed December 1, 2014. http://bbc.in/1b4ZdHc. And, David Folkenflik, "Social Media Allows Reports Despite Tehran's Curbs." NPR. June 16, 2009. Accessed December 1, 2014. http://n.pr/1Ev5rMx.

8. First reports of foreign journalists being expelled from Iran appeared on Twitter two days after the election results were announced: CPJ MENA, Twitter post, June 15, 2014, 7:50 AM. https://twitter.com/cpjmena/status/478187715683315712. And, "Iran Should Allow Journalists to Cover Opposition Rallies." Committee to Protect Journalists. June 17, 2009. Accessed December 1, 2014. http://bit.ly/1z3Fzqx.

9. For a list of tweets concerning journalists' arrests, see
http://bit.ly/1P4m4FA (Accessed December 1, 2014);
http://bit.ly/1H4uvwo (Accessed December 1, 2014);
http://bit.ly/1IllPrxJ (Accessed December 1, 2014);
http://bit.ly/1IllPzxf (Accessed December 1, 2014);
http://bit.ly/1P5dMxd (Accessed December 1, 2014);
http://bit.ly/1cbYgxK (Accessed December 1, 2014);
http://bit.ly/1DVrQOe (Accessed December 1, 2014).

Some still remain in prison five years later. See also CPJ MENA,
"Time to End a Five-year Crackdown in Iran (with Images,
Tweets)." *Storify*. June 10, 2014. Accessed April 26, 2015.
http://bit.ly/1GwgYul. And, Jason Stern, "Time to End a Five-year
Crackdown in Iran." Committee to Protect Journalists. June 10,
2014. Accessed December 1, 2014. http://cpj.org/x/5b7f.

10. "News from Iran - Tehran 30 July (8 Mordad)." YouTube.
July 30, 2009. Accessed December 1, 2014. http://bit.ly/1OWoaC1.
For a discussion of this transformation in media ecology, see Janet
A. Alexanian, "Eyewitness Accounts and Political Claims: Transnational Responses to the 2009 Postelection Protests in Iran," *Comparative Studies of South Asia Africa and the Middle East* 31:2 (2011):
425–442.

11. Roger Cohen, "A Journalist's 'Actual Responsibility.' "
New York Times. July 5, 2009. Accessed December 2, 2014.
http://nyti.ms/1KypG0z.

12. According to one source, "popular calls with instruction for
DDoS attacks were issued on social media and through mass
emails (that were kind of even more popular than social media at
some points.) In one example a bunch of students at Leiden University, Netherlands, targeted IRIB, Fars News, and Khamene'i's
website for about 2 or 3 hours using almost all the computers in
the main library at the University." See also Noah Shachtman,

"Activists Launch Hack Attacks on Tehran Regime." *Wired.* June 15, 2009. Accessed December 2, 2014. http://wrd.cm/1HIOoaH. And, Rob Faris and Rebekah Heacock, "Cracking Down on Digital Communication and Political Organizing in Iran." *OpenNet Initiative.* June 15, 2009. Accessed December 2, 2014. http://bit.ly/1DOBthQ.

13. These were later found to be mined by the government's newly purchased deep packet inspection equipment provided by a joint venture called Nokia Siemens Networks (NSN). See Christopher Rhoads, "Iran's Web Spying Aided by Western Technology." *Wall Street Journal.* June 22, 2009. Accessed April 26, 2015. http://on.wsj.com/1zdxAo5. Saeed Kamali Dehghan, "Iranian Consumers Boycott Nokia for 'collaboration.'" *The Guardian.* July 14, 2009. Accessed April 26, 2015. http://gu.com/p/29amv/stw. And Saeed Kamali Dehghan, "The Art of Protest in Iran." *The Guardian.* October 10, 2009. Accessed April 26, 2015. http://gu.com/p/2bbht/stw.

14. "Because all major media in Iran is state controlled, protesters found it difficult to coordinate demonstration meeting places and warn of clashes with police. Internet sites such as Twitter, YouTube, and Facebook became important for posting such information. The issue of authenticity came up repeatedly on these sites, as fears of government spies impersonating protesters and posting false information circulated online. In these cases, warnings were sent through 'trusted' Twitter users and postings on Facebook. The use of social media to mobilize within the country parallels the use of satellite television broadcasts (and their use of telephones and faxes) during the 2003 protests in Tehran." Alexanian, "Eyewitness Accounts and Political Claims," 432.

15. All domestic television and radio is state-run. Satellite television, which arrived in some Tehran neighborhoods in 1991, though prohibited since 1995, continues to provide alternatives to state programming.

16. "Iran Jamming BBC Persian." YouTube. June 17, 2009. Accessed April 26, 2015. http://bit.ly/1E9I49T. And, "BBC Persian 15 06 09." YouTube. June 15, 2009. Accessed April 26, 2015. http://bit.ly/1buCLIc.

17. Peter Horrocks, "Stop the Blocking Now." *BBC News.* June 14, 2009. Accessed April 26, 2015. http://bbc.in/rpvJ7Z.

18. Homa Maddah, "Nothing and No One Will Be the Same." *Tehran Avenue.* June 23, 2009. Accessed December 2, 2014. http://tehranavenue.com/article.php?id=885.

19. Alexanian, "Eyewitness Accounts and Political Claims," 430–431.

20. "Translation of Iran Slogans and Signs-2." *CNN iReport.* June 24, 2009. Accessed December 2, 2014. http://cnn.it/1zbrHem. And, "Translation of Iran Slogans and Signs." *CNN iReport.* June 22, 2009. Accessed December 2, 2014. http://cnn.it/1DVuZxf.

21. Chris Messina™, Twitter post, 23 Aug 2007, 12:25 PM. Accessed December 2, 2014. https://twitter.com/chrismessina/status/223115412.

22. Ben Parr, "Facebook Releases Persian Translation for #IranElection Crisis." *Mashable.* June 18, 2009. Accessed December 1, 2014. http://mashable.com/2009/06/18/facebook-persian. And, Yahya Kamalipour and Jonathan Acuff, eds., *Media, Power, and Politics in the Digital Age: The 2009 Presidential Election Uprising in Iran* (Lanham, MD: Rowman and Littlefield, 2010), 112.

23. Leena Rao, "Twitter Makes Hashtags More #Useful." *TechCrunch.* July 2, 2009. Accessed April 26, 2015. http://on.tcrn.ch/l/Rvdu.

24. Muhammad Hossein Panahi, *Jāmi'ah'shināsī-i shi'ārhā-yi inqilāb-i Islāmī-i Īrān* (Sociology of Slogans of Islamic Revolution) (Tehran: Institution of Contemporary Thought and Knowledge Press, 2004), 70.

25. Ibid., 42. September 8, 1978 (17 Shahrivar), also known as Black Friday, witnessed the death of many protestors by the Shah's army in Tehran, at Jaleh Square. The slogan "I will kill, I will kill, he who killed my brother" has its source in this demonstration. Jaleh Square was renamed Square of the Martyrs (Maidan-e Shohada). See "17 Shahrivar 1357 chant 'Mikosham, Mikosham, Anke Baradaram Kosht.'" YouTube. September 7, 2011. Accessed April 26, 2015. http://bit.ly/1bIy4eD.

26. First published in *Le Nouvel Observateur,* October 16–22, 1978. Translated and reproduced in Janet Afary and Kevin Anderson, *Foucault and the Iranian Revolution: Gender and the Seductions of Islamism* (Chicago: University of Chicago Press, 2005), 203–205.

27. Ibid., 205.

28. Ibid., 205.

29. Ranjana Khanna, "The Lumpenproletariat, the Subaltern, the Mental Asylum," *South Atlantic Quarterly* 112:1 (Winter 2013): 134.

30. Roxanne Varzi, "Iran's French Revolution: Religion, Philosophy, and Crowds," *ANNALS, AAPSS* 637 (September 2011): 59.

31. Elham Gheytanchi, "A Revolutionary Tradition: Shoars in Iranian Street Politics." *Words Without Borders.* September 18, 2009. Accessed April 26, 2015. http://bit.ly/1IcUY9X.

32. Ervand Abrahamian, "The Crowd in the Iranian Revolution," *Radical History Review* 105 (September 21, 2009): 23; parentheses mine.

33. For a discussion of this renaming, see Talinn Grigor, *Contemporary Iranian Art: From the Street to the Studio* (London: Reaktion Books, 2014), 40–41.

34. "8 Mordad (july/30/2009) Iran Part12." YouTube. July 30, 2009. Accessed December 2, 2014. http://youtu.be/PfEb7cydj68. "8 Mordad (july/30/2009) Iran Part13." YouTube. July 30, 2009. Accessed December 2, 2014. http://youtu.be/oRuNav6SJ-Y. "8 Mordad (july/30/2009) Iran Part5." YouTube. July 30, 2009. Accessed December 2, 2014. http://youtu.be/URRtAXorrE8.

"Iranian Police Arrest Mourners at Cemetery - 30 Jul 09."
YouTube. July 30, 2009. Accessed December 2, 2014.
http://youtu.be/4pohCrHD-n4. "Iran - Tehran Vali Asr St. - 30.Jul
Protests - P16." YouTube. July 30, 2009. Accessed December 2, 2014.
http://youtu.be/S1knl2T_LsA. "8 Mordad-valiasr-marg Bar Khamenei."
YouTube. July 30, 2009. Accessed December 2, 2014.
http://youtu.be/EwGOKeEYSA0.

35. "[Demonstration, Mordad 8th, Behesht-e Neda]." YouTube.
July 30, 2009. Accessed April 26, 2015. http://bit.ly/1DqzzDG.

36. For a discussion of the plan and significance of the cemetery, see Grigor, *Contemporary Iranian Art*, 66–67.

37. "Updates from 8 Mordad (30 July)." PBS. July 30, 2009.
Accessed December 2, 2014. http://to.pbs.org/1E9G8hJ.

38. As Roxanne Varzi argues, "During the Islamic Revolution,
crowds chanted 'Down with the Shah'; during the Green Movement, the chant became, 'Down with the dictator.' This is no simple double entendre but a very clear pronouncement that the Iranian demonstrators were not advocating a return to monarchial
Iran, nor were they accepting the current presidency. This was an
important move, given the support that came from the diaspora in
the United States, some of whom took the opportunity to demon-
strate 'alongside' Iranians in Iran, while subtly promoting their own
desires to return to a monarchial past. What the Iranian diaspora
and the Western press did not understand is that Iranians in Iran
had no intention of throwing the baby out with the bath-water. If
anything, they were looking for a way to salvage their religion rather
than allow it to sink with a failing state. Despite the disillusionment
with an Islamic government, most Iranians, especially the youth
who were born after the revolution, still find comfort and a need for
a sense of some kind of spirituality in the face of a failing economy,
a poor education system, and rampant depression." Varzi, "Iran's
French Revolution," 60–61.

39. "How Iran's Opposition Inverts Old Slogans." *BBC News*.
July 12, 2009. Accessed December 2, 2014. http://bbc.in/1JIvMqk.

40. "[Quds Day Demonstration - Tehran, Karim Khan St. towards Valiasr Sq.]." YouTube. September 24, 2009. Accessed December 2, 2014. http://youtu.be/wc4dZimPDok.

41. Hypercities Earth. Accessed December 2, 2014. http://hypercities.ats.ucla.edu/.

42. The recording was later made available by Mehdi Saharkhiz over a compilation of digital videos from the Quds Day demonstrations here: "Breaking News: Sephah's Leaked Radio on Ghods Day September 18 09." YouTube. September 21, 2009. Accessed December 2, 2014. http://youtu.be/GoPhDrGAzn4.

43. "[Quds Day Demonstration - Tehran, Karim Khan St. towards Valiasr Sq.]." YouTube. And, "[Quds Day - Tehran, Karim Khan St. From 7th Tir Sq. towards Valiasr]." YouTube. September 24, 2009. Accessed December 2, 2014. http://youtu.be/nwB5p7qS9r4.

44. "[Quds Day Demonstration - Tehran, Karim Khan St. towards Valiasr Sq.]." YouTube.

45. "The chant of 'Allahu akbar' and other gestures and words have been used for thirty years to sustain the political imagination of the revolutionary state. Redeploying them to question the elections, crowds challenge the order of things through its own vocabulary." See Setrag Manoukian, "Where Is this Place? Crowds, Audio-vision, and Poetry in Postelection Iran," *Public Culture* 22:2 (2010): 246.

46. Minoo Moallem, *Between Warrior Brother and Veiled Sister: Islamic Fundamentalism and the Politics of Patriarchy in Iran* (Berkeley: University of California Press, 2005), 85.

47. Ibid.

48. Gheytanchi, "Revolutionary Tradition."

49. The term became common usage in slogans and in protests convened against Ahmadinejad's presidency. It was added to Wikepedia in July 2009. See Robert Tait, "The Dust Revolution—How Mahmoud Ahmadinejad's Jibe Backfired." *The Guardian*. Accessed December 2, 2014. http://gu.com/p/28jb9/stw.

50. The torn overcoat is a reference to Ahmadinejad's unkept appearances. Summer or winter, he was always seen pictured in one of his overcoats.

51. Gheytanchi, "Revolutionary Tradition."

52. For a discussion of the city as metaphor in Benjamin, see Miriam Hansen, "Benjamin, Cinema and Experience: The Blue Flower in the Land of Technology," *New German Critique* 40 (Winter 1987): 194–195.

53. Walter Benjamin, "The Return of the Flâneur." *Selected Writings II Part 1 1927–1930*, trans. Rodney Livingstone et al., ed. Michael W. Jennings, Howard Eiland, and Gary Smith (Cambridge, MA: Harvard University Press, 1999), 264.

54. Hansen, "Benjamin, Cinema and Experience," 194–195.

55. Walter Benjamin, "Doctrine of the Similar," *New German Critique* 17 (1979): 65.

56. Susan Buck-Morss, "Walter Benjamin Revolutionary Writer II," *New Left Review* 129 (September–October 1981): 85–86.

57. Ibid.

58. Ibid., 78.

II. MEME

1. Persiankiwi, Twitter post, June 23, 2009, 9:09 AM. Accessed December 1, 2014. https://twitter.com/persiankiwi/status/2294171672.

2. "In what may be another sign that Iran's authorities are trying to disrupt opposition protests online, a blogger using the screen name 'mms7778' has taken to posting this update every minute on Twitter: #iranelection Ahmadinejad The President. Man with clear judgment. Will be inaugurated soon again. The same blogger posts obscene insults attacking Iran's opposition supporters in between each repetition of his praise for Mr. Ahmadinejad. By using the tag '#iranelection' in each update, this anonymous blogger ensures that people searching Twitter for news of the protests will continuously encounter these insults." Robert Mackey, "July 20:

Updates on the Protests in Iran." *New York Times.* July 21, 2009. Accessed April 26, 2015. http://nyti.ms/1OtpMIz. See also Mike Masnick, "Iran Sends Warning SMS Messages to Potential Protestors." *Techdirt.* June 16, 2010. Accessed April 26, 2015. http://bit.ly/1b4zZbW. And, Christopher Rhoads, "Iran's Web Spying Aided by Western Technology." *Wall Street Journal.* June 22, 2009. Accessed April 26, 2015. http://on.wsj.com/1zdxA05. Saeed Kamali Dehghan, "Iranian Consumers Boycott Nokia for 'collaboration.'" *The Guardian.* July 14, 2009. Accessed April 26, 2015. http://gu.com/p/29amv/stw. And Saeed Kamali Dehghan, "The Art of Protest in Iran." *The Guardian.* October 10, 2009. Accessed April 26, 2015. http://gu.com/p/2bbht/stw.

3. Richard Dawkins, *The Selfish Gene* (Oxford, UK: Oxford University Press, 2006), 192.

4. Olivia Solon, "Richard Dawkins on the Internet's Hijacking of the Word 'meme.'" *WebCite.* June 20, 2013. Accessed December 1, 2014. http://www.webcitation.org/6HzDGE9Go.

5. For further images of these practices, see http://divarnevis.wordpress.com/ (accessed December 1, 2014).

6. Persiankiwi, Twitter post, June 16, 2009, 11:40 AM. Accessed December 1, 2014. https://twitter.com/persiankiwi/statuses/2195843826. See also Persiankiwi, Twitter post, June 18, 2009, 3:56 PM. Accessed December 1, 2014. https://twitter.com/persiankiwi/statuses/2229598414.

7. Mackey, "July 20." See also Tara Mahtafar, "Gearing Up for 13 Aban." PBS. November 2, 2009. April 26, 2015. http://to.pbs.org/1zb5cGi.

8. Mossadegh would never forget the people who died on that bloody day. In his will he requested that he be buried in the cemetery belonging to the martyrs of 30 Tir. This wish was not granted.

9. "Amid Crackdown, Iranians Try a Shocking Protest." *Time.* July 22, 2009. Accessed April 26, 2015. http://ti.me/PFqzTB.

10. "Arrests at New Iranian Protests." *BBC News.* July 21, 2009. Accessed April 26, 2015. http://bbc.in/1HL5Iol.

11. Mackey, "July 20."

12. Persiankiwi, Twitter post, June 23, 2009, 3:06 AM. Accessed December 1, 2014. https://twitter.com/persiankiwi/status/2292737838. And, "Shiraz, Iran, June 21, 2009 Car Protesters." YouTube. June 22, 2009. Accessed April 26, 2015. http://bit.ly/1buGXHP.

13. "Iran in August 01 2009—[Chalous Rd] Parts 1-4." YouTube. August 1, 2009. Accessed April 26, 2015. http://bit.ly/1QxDh8B and http://bit.ly/1zba8Lo and http://bit.ly/1J1OGsb.

14. "Green Movement Balloon." YouTube. June 26, 2009. Accessed December 1, 2014. http://bit.ly/1PIcHbD. See also "[Green Balloons with Images of Our Beloved Departed]." YouTube. June 23, 2010. Accessed December 1, 2014. http://bit.ly/1E9PWby and "July 4: Bring out the balloons". Standing with Free Iran. July 2, 2009. Accessed April 26, 2015. http://bit.ly/1JtPCsA.

15. Andy Borowitz, "Ayatollah Warns Iranians: 'I Am Following You All on Twitter.'" *Huffington Post.* June 19, 2009. Accessed December 1, 2014. http://huff.to/ldvrnB.

16. Rahaf Harfoush, "#IranElections & Acts of Corporate Good – Rahaf Harfoush – Strategist & NYT Best Selling Author." *Rahaf Harfoush.* Accessed December 1, 2014. http://bit.ly/1OtKnfZ.

17. Elise Labott, "State Department to Twitter: Keep Iranian Tweets Coming." *Anderson Cooper 360.* June 16, 2009. Accessed December 1, 2014. http://cnn.it/1DAi2dq.

18. Ben Parr, "Facebook Releases Persian Translation for #Iran Election Crisis." *Mashable.* June 18, 2009. Accessed December 1, 2014. http://mashable.com/2009/06/18/facebook-persian/.

19. Franz Och, "Google Translates Persian." *Official Google Blog.* June 18, 2009. Accessed December 1, 2014. http://bit.ly/1b4LBMm.

20. Kathy Riordan, "How Twitter and #Iranelection Changed Each Other." *Open Salon.* June 8, 2010. Accessed December 1, 2014. http://bit.ly/1zuyzDA.

21. Harold Nolte. "Google Logo for Iran: Vote Update." *Examiner*. June 21, 2009. Accessed December 1, 2014. http://bit.ly/1GSEtM7. Follow link: http://bit.ly/1AJAA9U. See also Persiankiwi, Twitter post, June 18, 2009, 7:41 AM. Accessed December 1, 2014. https://twitter.com/persiankiwi/status/2222973582.

22. Setareh Sabety, "Graphic Content: Semiotics of a Youtube uprising," in *Media, Power, and Politics in the Digital Age: The 2009 Presidential Election Uprising in Iran*, ed. Kamalipour Yahya and Jonathan Acuff (Lanham, MD: Rowman & Littlefield, 2010), 119–124.

23. Marwan M. Kraidy and Sara Mourad, "Hypermedia Space and Global Communications Studies: Lessons from the Middle East," *Global Media Journal* 9:16 (2009): article 8.

24. Krista Mahr, "The Top 10 Everything of 2009." *Time*. December 8, 2009. Accessed December 1, 2014. http://ti.me/13YcywV. On commemorating Neda's death, see "Updates from 8 Mordad (30 July)." PBS. July 30, 2009. Accessed December 1, 2014. http://to.pbs.org/1bIF4bh.

25. Hajatoleslam Mohammad Motahhari is the son of Morteza Motahhari, a close ally of Ayatollah Khomeini during the Iranian Revolution.

26. Daniel Nasaw and Matthew Weaver, "Iran Protests to Honour the Dead." *The Guardian*. July 30, 2009. Accessed December 1, 2014. http://www.theguardian.com/news/blog/2009/jul/30/iran-protest.

27. Setareh Sabety, "40 Days Ago We Died." PBS. July 31, 2009. Accessed December 1, 2014. http://to.pbs.org/1OW2FBp.

28. Asked about the uses of social media in the #iranelection crisis, the social media guru Clay Shirky responded: "I'm always a little reticent to draw lessons from things still unfolding, but it seems pretty clear that . . . this is it. The big one. This is the first revolution that has been catapulted onto a global stage and transformed by social media. I've been thinking a lot about the Chicago demonstrations of 1968 where they chanted 'the whole world is watching.' Really, that wasn't true then. But this time it's true . . . and people throughout the world are not only listening

but responding. They're engaging with individual participants, they're passing on their messages to their friends, and they're even providing detailed instructions to enable web proxies allowing Internet access that the authorities can't immediately censor. That kind of participation is really extraordinary." Chris Anderson, "Q&A with Clay Shirky on Twitter and Iran." *TED Blog.* June 16, 2009. Accessed December 1, 2014. http://wp.me/p10512-aBH.

29. Helen Kennedy, "President Obama Calls Iranian Martyr Neda's Death 'Heartbreaking.'" *NY Daily News.* June 23, 2009. Accessed December 1, 2014. http://nydn.us/1HIBIR8.

30. "Jon Bon Jovi, Andy Perform 'Stand By Me' for Iran." RadioFreeEurope/RadioLiberty. June 29, 2009. Accessed December 1, 2014. http://bit.ly/1DAmkRW.

31. "Joan Baez, 'We Shall Overcome' (2009)." YouTube. June 25, 2009. Accessed December 1, 2014. http://bit.ly/1z3rWHY.

32. Emad Zande Vakil, "Madonna's Tribute to Iran's Green Movement." A Forum on Human Rights and Democracy in Iran. July 10, 2009. Accessed December 1, 2014. http://bit.ly/1IcZUfo.

33. Barack Obama, "Remarks by the President on Winning the Nobel Peace Prize." The White House. October 9, 2009. Accessed December 1, 2014. http://www.whitehouse.gov/the_press_office/ Remarks-by-the-President-on-Winning-the-Nobel-Peace-Prize.

34. Nasaw and Weaver, "Iran Protests to Honour the Dead."

35. NedaSpeaks.org, "Neda." YouTube. June 7, 2010. Accessed December 1, 2014. http://bit.ly/1HLk9S1.

36. "We Are Neda." Accessed December 1, 2014. http://neda.webnode.com/.

37. Established in 2009 in the aftermath of the crisis, the organization today is made up of a team of creatives, activists, and lawyers that energetically seek the release of political prisoners, open access to information and technology, the reform of Iranian laws in accord with human rights, free and fair elections, and that insist on a moratorium on the death penalty until due process rights are

guaranteed in Iran. http://united4iran.org/; Julia Ritchey, "Global Protests Call for End to Iran's Post-Election Crackdown." Payvand Iran News. July 27, 2009. Accessed April 27, 2015. http://www.payvand.com/news/09/jul/1245.html. "A Year Ago Today: July 25th Global Day of Action." UnitedforIran. Accessed April 27, 2015. http://bit.ly/1DEpZyg; Flickr stream: https://flic.kr/s/aHsjn8RtwV.

38. Reza Deghati (photographer). Luna4Freedom. Accessed December 1, 2014. http://luna4freedom.files.wordpress.com/2010/01/reza_deghati1.jpg.

39. Mazyar Lotfalian, "Aestheticized Politics, Visual Culture, and Emergent Forms of Digital Practice," *International Journal of Communication* 7 (2013): 1388.

40. Ibid., 1371.

41. Minoo Moallem, *Between Warrior Brother and Veiled Sister: Islamic Fundamentalism and the Politics of Patriarchy in Iran* (Berkeley: University of California Press, 2005), 89–90.

42. Mazyar Lotfalian, "Aestheticized Politics," 1371.

43. Ibid., 1373.

44. Ibid., 1381.

45. Moallem, *Between Warrior Brother and Veiled Sister,* 85.

46. Reza Deghati, "Neda of Ashura." YouTube. December 25, 2009. Accessed December 4, 2014. http://bit.ly/1Gwaz2g.

47. Persiankiwi, Twitter post, June 20, 2009, 7:41 AM. Accessed March 21, 2015. https://twitter.com/persiankiwi/status/2259390877.

48. Jonathan Sterne, *The Audible Past: Cultural Origins of Sound Reproduction* (Durham, NC: Duke University Press, 2003), 291.

49. "Translation of Iran Slogans and Signs-2." *CNN iReport.* June 24, 2009. Accessed December 1, 2014. http://cnn.it/1zbrHem.

50. Walter Benjamin, *Berlin Childhood around 1900* (Boston: Harvard University Press, 2006), 50.

51. Avital Ronell, *The Telephone Book, Technology, Schizophrenia, Electric Speech* (Lincoln: University of Nebraska Press, 1989), 438.

52. Homa Maddah, "Nothing and No One Will Be the Same." *Tehran Avenue.* June 23, 2009. Accessed December 1, 2014. http://tehranavenue.com/article.php?id=885.

53. Setrag Manoukian, "Where Is This Place? Crowds, Audiovision, and Poetry in Postelection Iran," *Public Culture* 22:2 (2010): 241.

54. Ibid.

55. Moallem, *Between Warrior Brother and Veiled Sister,* 85.

56. Manoukian, "Where Is This Place?" 238.

57. "Inja Kojast Inja Iran Ast Sarzamine Man O To." YouTube. June 19, 2009. Accessed December 1, 2014. https://www.youtube.com/watch?v=2oM6l9PO6Yo. For more rooftop videos, see "Iran: The Rooftop Project." MightierThan.com. July 10, 2009. Accessed December 1, 2014. http://bit.ly/1bINmzZ. See also Manoukian, "Where Is This Place?" 251–252. I have modified some of Manoukian's translations.

58. Manoukian, "Where Is This Place?" 240.

59. Ibid., 237.

60. Ibid., 254.

61. "Khodaya Khob Gosh Kon Agar Khabidi Bidar Sho Daran Sedat Mikonan." YouTube. July 5, 2009. Accessed December 1, 2014. https://www.youtube.com/watch?v=o6SjFq2xTIo. See also Manoukian, "Where Is This Place?" 254–256. I have made some minor changes to Manoukian's translations.

62. For a discussion of the preservation and canning of sound alongside the embalmment of the dead and the canning of food in the era of industrialization, see Sterne, *Audible Past,* especially the final chapter, "A Resonant Tomb."

63. Quoted in John Mowitt, *Radio: Essays in Bad Reception* (Berkeley: University of California Press, 2011), 93.

64. Ibid., 94.

65. Jalal Al-i Ahmad, *Occidentosis: A Plague from the West,* trans. R. Campbell (Berkeley, CA: Mizan Press, 1962/1984).

66. Much of this is developed in my close readings of the Iranian cinema of the postrevolutionary period in *Displaced Allegories: Post-Revolutionary Iranian Cinema* (Durham, NC: Duke University Press, 2008).

67. Henri Corbin, "Mundus Imaginalis" (May 1964). Hermetic Library. Accessed December 1, 2014. http://hermetic.com/moorish/mundus-imaginalis.html.

68. Miriam Bratu Hansen, "Room-for-Play: Benjamin's Gamble with Cinema," *October* 109 (Summer 2004): 3–45.

III. SELFIE

1. Persiankiwi, Twitter post, June 18, 2009, 11:46 AM. Accessed November 30, 2014. https://twitter.com/persiankiwi/status/2226295657.

2. "The Media Mix-up That Ruined My Life." *BBC News*. Accessed November 30, 2014. http://www.bbc.com/news/magazine-20267989. "Not that 'Neda': How the Wrong Photo Became an Icon." *Modernist Times Post*. June 24, 2009. Accessed April 27, 2015. http://bit.ly/1HMnbW8.

3. "Transcript: Obama's Press Conference." *CBSNews*. Accessed November 30, 2014. http://www.cbsnews.com/news/transcript-obamas-press-conference.

4. Scott Wilson, "Obama Reverses Pledge to Release Photos of Detainee Abuse." *Washington Post*. May 14, 2009. Accessed November 30, 2014. http://wapo.st/1dhJvdu.

5. Ziba Mir-Hosseini, "Broken Taboos in Post-Election Iran." Middle East Research and Information Project. December 17, 2009. Accessed November 30, 2014. http://www.merip.org/mero/mero121709.

6. For reference see footnote 39 of Walter Benjamin's "Work of Art in the Age of Reproducibility (Third Version)."

7. See Ian Balfour, "Reversal, Quotation (Benjamin's History)," *MLN* 106:3, German Issue (April 1991): 637.

8. Haleh Anvari, "The Fetish of Staring at Iran's Women." *New York Times*. June 16, 2014. Accessed November 30, 2014. http://nyti.ms/1p91tz6

9. Ibid.

10. The coup against Mossadegh was soon to be used as a blueprint for many other CIA coups throughout the world—beginning with the overthrow of Jacobo Arbenz in Guatemala ten months later.

11. Morad Shirin, "Student Day in Iran: Breaking the Climate of Fear and Intimidation." Yahoo! Groups. December 12, 2006. Accessed November 30, 2014. https://groups.yahoo.com/neo/groups/MESN/conversations/topics/9029.

12. "Tehran Student Protests in Amateur Pictures." *The Observers*. July 12, 2009. Accessed November 30, 2014. http://f24.my/1A2ZSj5.

13. Mir-Hosseini, "Broken Taboos in Post-Election Iran." A video-recording of Majid Tavakoli's speech and some highlights from are transcribed in English here: "Majid Tavakoli's brave speech on 16 Azar 87 Tehran University." YouTube. December 17, 2009. Accessed April 26, 2015. https://youtu.be/vb3QNxdoK2A.

14. The YouTube video made during the first week of the campaign captures the spread of the #IamMajid campaign across the globe: "We Are All Majid Tavakoli." YouTube. December 10, 2009. Accessed December 5, 2014. http://bit.ly/1A302a4.

15. Sara Mameni, "Conceptualizing Loss: US feminism and the Iranian Revolution" Unpublished paper presented at the Middle Eastern Studies Annual Conference in Washington, DC, November 2014.

16. Ranjana Khanna, *Algeria Cuts: Women and Representation, 1830 to the Present* (Stanford, CA: Stanford University Press, 2008), 168.

17. Ibid., 148.

18. Mameni, "Conceptualizing Loss."

19. See Negar Mottahedeh, "Mutilated Body of the Modern Nation: Qurrat Al-'Ayn's Unveiling and the Persian Massacre of the Bábís." Bahai Library Online. January 1, 1998. Accessed November 30, 2014. http://bit.ly/1GxJpLw. And, Negar Mottahedeh, "Ruptured Spaces and Effective Histories: The Unveiling of the Babi Poetess Qurrat Al-`Ayn Tahirih in the Gardens of Badasht." Cornell Library. January 1, 1998. Accessed November 30, 2014. http://bit.ly/1b4Tykr.

20. 'Abdu'l-Bahá Abbas, *The Promulgation of Universal Peace: Talks Delivered by 'Abdu'l-Bahá during His Visit to the United States and Canada in 1912*, 2nd. ed. (Wilmette: Bahá'í Publishing Trust, 1982), 74–77. See also, Negar Mottahedeh, *'Abdu'l-Bahá's Journey West: The Course of Human Solidarity* (New York: Palgrave Macmillan, 2013).

21. Golnaz Esfandiari, "Iran's Nobel Peace Laureate Praises 'Men In Hijabs' Campaign." RadioFreeEurope/RadioLiberty. December 16, 2009. Accessed November 30, 2014. http://bit.ly/1DB6gzs.

22. Anvari, "The Fetish of Staring at Iran's Women."

23. Others memed the faces of Iranian Supreme Leader Ayatollah Khamanei and President Mahmud Ahmadinejad into Majid Tavakoli's veiled image: "Be a Man." *Know Your Meme News.* Accessed December 5, 2014. http://knowyourmeme.com/memes/events/be-a-man.

24. Julian Stallabrass, "On Selfies." *London Review of Books.* June 5, 2014. Accessed November 30, 2014. http://bit.ly/1oyS9aL.

25. Rebecca L. Stein, "Selfie Militarism." *London Review of Books.* May 23, 2014. Accessed November 30, 2014. http://www.lrb.co.uk/blog/2014/05/23/rebecca-l-stein/selfie-militarism-2/; and Adi Kuntsman and Rebecca L. Stein, Digital Militarism: Israel's Occupation in the Age of Social Media (Stanford, CA: Stanford University Press, 2015).

26. Stallabrass, "On Selfies."

27. Ibid.

28. Setrag Manoukian, "Where Is This Place? Crowds, Audio-vision, and Poetry in Postelection Iran," *Public Culture* 22:2 (2010): 243–245.

29. In fact, opposition to calling "the people" "*Kash-o-khak*" (riff-raff) was so acerbic that it entered common parlance and was added to Wikipedia in early July 2009. http://bit.ly/1Id9H4Q; Robert Tait, "The Dust Revolution—How Mahmoud Ahmadinejad's Jibe Backfired." *The Guardian*. June 18, 2009. Accessed April 27, 2015. http://gu.com/p/28jb9/stw.

30. Manoukian, "Where Is This Place?" 243–245.

31. See, for example, the report at 4:44 p.m. on July 30, 2009: http://www.theguardian.com/news/blog/2009/jul/30/iran-protest (accessed November 30, 2014); and the early report of unconfirmed defection in the ranks of the Revolutionary Guard in @persiankiwi's tweets https://twitter.com/persiankiwi/status/2229598414 (accessed November 30, 2014).

32. The published interview that was based on these conversations appeared online on the "Tehran Bureau" site. It was subsequently translated and published in "Madreseye Feministi." An earlier draft of this section was posted in Persian translation on the BBC Persian website on the occasion of International Women's Day, 2011: Golbarg Bashi and Negar Mottahedeh, "Picturing Ourselves: 1953, 1979 and 2009, A Conversation with Negar Mottahedeh." Tehran Bureau. July 2, 2009. Accessed November 30, 2014. http://www.pbs.org/wgbh/pages/frontline/tehranbureau/2009/07/picturing-ourselves-1953-1979-and-2009.html. See also http://www.feministschool.org/spip.php?article5099 (accessed November 30, 2014) and http://www.bbc.co.uk/persian/iran/2011/03/110310_l25_mottahedeh_women_day_iwd2011.shtml (accessed November 30, 2014).

33. Some of the images I read closely in this section are different from the ones used for the interview.

34. Tom Heneghan, "Notes on France's Ban-the-burqa Debate." *FaithWorld*. July 3, 2009. Accessed November 30, 2014. http://reut.rs/1pgVeca. And, Natalie Orenstein, "France Hardly

Alone on Burqa Ban." *Newsdesk*. July 21, 2010. Accessed November 30, 2014. http://bit.ly/1HIGXQN.

35. Manoukian, "Where Is This Place?" 249.

36. As "a liveness" that must be regarded, as Esther Hammelburg argues, a "historically defined construct that hinges on the potential connection, through media, to events that matter to us as they unfold." For a thoughtful discussion of liveness as a configuration of affinity and immediacy, see Esther Hammelburg, "#stemfie: Reconceptualising Liveness in the Era of Social Media" (forthcoming in *Tidschrift voor Mediageschiedenis*); and R. Vianello, "The Power Politics of 'Live' Television," *Journal of Film and Video* 37:3 (1985): 26–40; N. Couldry, "Liveness, 'Reality,' and the Mediated Habitus from Television to the Mobile Phone," *Communication Review* 7:4 (2004): 353–361; P. Auslander, "Digital Liveness: A Historico-philosophical Perspective," *PAJ: A Journal of Performance and Art* 34:3 (2012): 3–11.

37. Ibid., 247.

38. Ibid., 249.

39. See also video "Iranian public demonstrations in favor of nationalizing Anglo-Iranian Oil Company HD Stock Footage." YouTube. June 5, 2015. Accessed April 25, 2015. https://youtu.be/FuJACECof2g. Hollywood star Rita Hayworth's popularity in Iran stemmed in part from her marriage to the Iranian Prince Ali (Aly Khan) Salman Aga Khan in 1949.

40. Sophie Kier, a Canadian journalist, was Millett's travel companion in Iran.

41. Negar Mottahedeh, *Displaced Allegories: Post-Revolutionary Iranian Cinema* (Durham, NC: Duke University Press, 2008).

42. Mir-Hosseini, "Broken Taboos in Post-Election Iran."

43. Damien McElroy and Ahmad Vahdat, "Suntanned Women to Be Arrested under Islamic Dress Code." *The Telegraph*. April 27, 2010. Accessed November 30, 2014. http://bit.ly/1buObM5.

44. "Iran's Morality Police: Patrolling the Streets by Stealth." *The Guardian*. June 19, 2014. Accessed November 30, 2014. http://gu.com/p/3q8b9/stw.

45. Pardis Mahdavi discusses this in *Passionate Uprising: Iran's Sexual Revolution* (Stanford, CA: Stanford University Press, 2008).

46. Khanna, *Algeria Cuts,* 147.

47. "Selfie Culture a New Battleground for the Iranian Regime." *The Guardian.* June 13, 2014. Accessed November 30, 2014. http://gu.com/p/3q3my/stw.

48. Mir-Hosseini, "Broken Taboos in Post-Election Iran."

49. Ibid.

50. Joan Copjec, "The Object-gaze, Shame, Hejab, Cinema." *Filozofski Vestnik* 27:2 (2006): 11–29.

51. Hamid Dabashi, "La Vita Nuda: Baring Bodies, Bearing Witness." *Aljazeera.* January 23, 2012. Accessed November 30, 2014. http://bit.ly/1H2NAfu.

52. Pierre Dardot and Christian Laval, *The New Way of the World: On Neoliberal Society* (New York: Verso, 2014).

53. Jacques Rancière, *Dissensus: On Politics and Aesthetics,* trans. Steven Corcoran (New York: Continuum, 2010), 37–38.

54. Dabashi, "La Vita Nuda."

55. Peter Beaumont, "The Truth about Twitter, Facebook and the Uprisings in the Arab World." *The Guardian.* February 25, 2011. Accessed December 1, 2014. http://gu.com/p/2nbnk/stw.

56. Noam Chomsky, "The Cairo-Madison Connection." *Truth Out.* March 9, 2011. Accessed April 26, 2015. http://www.truth-out.org/the-cairo-madison-connection68333 or http://truth-out.org/archive/component/k2/item/94854:the-cairomadison-connection.

FURTHER READING

'Abdu'l-Bahá Abbas. *The Promulgation of Universal Peace: Talks Delivered by 'Abdu'l-Bahá during His Visit to the United States and Canada in 1912*, 2nd ed. (Wilmette, IL: Bahá'í Publishing Trust, 1982).

Abrahamian, Ervand. "The Crowd in the Iranian Revolution." *Radical History Review* 105 (September 21, 2009).

Afary, Janet, and Kevin Anderson. *Foucault and the Iranian Revolution: Gender and the Seductions of Islamism* (Chicago: University of Chicago Press, 2005).

Alexanian, Janet A. "Eyewitness Accounts and Political Claims: Transnational Responses to the 2009 Postelection Protests in Iran." *Comparative Studies of South Asia Africa and the Middle East* 31:2 (2011): 425–442.

Auslander, P. "Digital Liveness: A Historico-philosophical Perspective." *PAJ: A Journal of Performance and Art* 34:3 (2012): 3–11.

Balfour, Ian. "Reversal, Quotation (Benjamin's History)." *MLN* 106:3, German Issue (April 1991): 622–647.

Benjamin, Walter. *Berlin Childhood Around 1900* (Boston: Harvard University Press, 2006).

———. "Doctrine of the Similar." *New German Critique* 17 (1979): 65–69.

————. *Selected Writings II 1927–1930*, trans. Rodney Livingstone et al., ed. Michael W. Jennings, Howard Eiland, and Gary Smith (Cambridge, MA: Harvard University Press, 1999).

————. "Work of Art in the Age of Reproducibility (Third Version)." In *Selected Writings IV (1939–1940)*, trans. Rodney Livingstone et al., ed. Marcus Bullock, Michael W. Jennings, Howard Eiland, et al. (Cambridge, MA: Harvard University Press, 1996), 251–283.

Buck-Morss, Susan. "Walter Benjamin Revolutionary Writer II." *New Left Review* 129 (September–October 1981): 77–95.

Cohen, Roger. "A Journalist's 'Actual Responsibility.'" *New York Times*, July 5, 2009. http://nyti.ms/1KypGoz (accessed December 2, 2014).

Copjec, Joan. "The Object-gaze, Shame, Hejab, Cinema." *Filozofski Vestnik* 27:2 (2006): 11–29.

Corbin, Henry. "Mundus Imaginalis" (May 1964). Hermetic Library. http://hermetic.com/moorish/mundus-imaginalis.html (accessed December 1, 2014).

Couldry, N. "Liveness, 'Reality,' and the Mediated Habitus from Television to the Mobile Phone." *Communication Review* 7:4 (2004): 353–361.

Dardot, Pierre, and Christian Laval. *The New Way of the World: On Neoliberal Society* (New York: Verso, 2014).

Dawkins, Richard. *The Selfish Gene* (Oxford, UK: Oxford University Press, 2006).

Gheytanchi, Elham. "A Revolutionary Tradition: Shoars in Iranian Street Politics." *Words Without Borders*, September 18, 2009. http://wordswithoutborders.org/article/a-revolutionary-tradition-shoars-in-iranian-street-politics (accessed December 1, 2014).

Grigor, Talinn. *Contemporary Iranian Art: From the Street to the Studio* (London: Reaktion Books, 2014).

Hammelburg, Esther. "#stemfie: Reconceptualising Liveness in the Era of Social Media." Forthcoming in *Tidschrift voor Mediageschiedenis*.

Hansen, Miriam. "Benjamin, Cinema and Experience: The Blue Flower in the Land of Technology." *New German Critique* 40 (Winter 1987): 179–224.

———. "Room-for-Play: Benjamin's Gamble with Cinema." *October* 109 (Summer 2004): 3–45.

Kamalipour, Yahya, and Jonathan Acuff, eds. *Media, Power, and Politics in the Digital Age: The 2009 Presidential Election Uprising in Iran* (Lanham, MD: Rowman & Littlefield, 2010).

Khanna, Ranjana. *Algeria Cuts: Women and Representation, 1830 to the Present* (Stanford, CA: Stanford University Press, 2008).

———. "The Lumpenproletariat, the Subaltern, the Mental Asylum." *South Atlantic Quarterly* 112:1 (Winter 2013): 129–143.

Kraidy, Marwan M., and Sara Mourad. "Hypermedia Space and Global Communications Studies: Lessons from the Middle East." *Global Media Journal* 9:16 (2009): 1–19.

Lotfalian, Mazyar. "Aestheticized Politics, Visual Culture, and Emergent Forms of Digital Practice." *International Journal of Communication* 7 (2013): 1371–1390.

Mahdavi, Pardis. *Passionate Uprising: Iran's Sexual Revolution* (Stanford, CA: Stanford University Press, 2008).

Mameni, Sara. "Conceptualizing Loss: US Feminism and the Iranian Revolution." Unpublished paper presented at the Middle Eastern Studies Annual Conference in Washington, DC, November 2014.

Manoukian, Setrag. "Where Is This Place? Crowds, Audio-vision, and Poetry in Postelection Iran." *Public Culture* 22:2 (2010): 237–263.

Mir-Hosseini, Ziba. "Broken Taboos in Post-Election Iran." *Middle East Research and Information Project*, December 17, 2009. http://www.merip.org/mero/mero121709 (accessed November 30, 2014).

Moallem, Minoo. *Between Warrior Brother and Veiled Sister: Islamic Fundamentalism and the Politics of Patriarchy in Iran* (Berkeley: University of California Press, 2005).

Mottahedeh, Negar. *Displaced Allegories: Post-Revolutionary Iranian Cinema* (Durham, NC: Duke University Press, 2008).

———. *'Abdu'l-Bahá's Journey West: The Course of Human Solidarity* (New York: Palgrave Macmillan, 2013).

Mowitt, John. Radio*: Essays in Bad Reception* (Berkeley: University of California Press, 2011).

Panahi, Muhammad Hossein. *Jāmi'ah'shināsī-i shi'ārhā-yi inqilāb-i Islāmī-i Īrān* (Sociology of slogans of the Islamic Revolution) (Tehran: Institution of Contemporary Thought and Knowledge Press, 2004).

Rancière, Jacques. *Dissensus: On Politics and Aesthetics*, trans. Steven Corcoran (New York: Continuum, 2010).

Ronell, Avital. *The Telephone Book, Technology, Schizophrenia, Electric Speech* (Lincoln: University of Nebraska Press, 1989).

Sabety, Setareh. "Graphic Content: Semiotics of a YouTube Uprising." In *Media, Power, and Politics in the Digital Age: The 2009 Presidential Election Uprising in Iran*, ed. Kamalipour Yahya and Jonathan Acuff (Lanham, MD: Rowman & Littlefield, 2010), 119–124.

Stein, Rebecca L. "Selfie Militarism." *LRB*, May 23, 2014. http://bit.ly/1bC2m1F (accessed November 30, 2014).

Sterne, Jonathan. *The Audible Past: Cultural Origins of Sound Reproduction* (Durham, NC: Duke University Press, 2003).

Varzi, Roxanne. "Iran's French Revolution: Religion, Philosophy, and Crowds." *ANNALS, AAPSS* 637 (September 2011): 53–63.

Vianello, R. "The Power Politics of 'Live' Television." *Journal of Film and Video* 37:3 (1985): 26–40.